Amazing Animals

COLORING BOOK

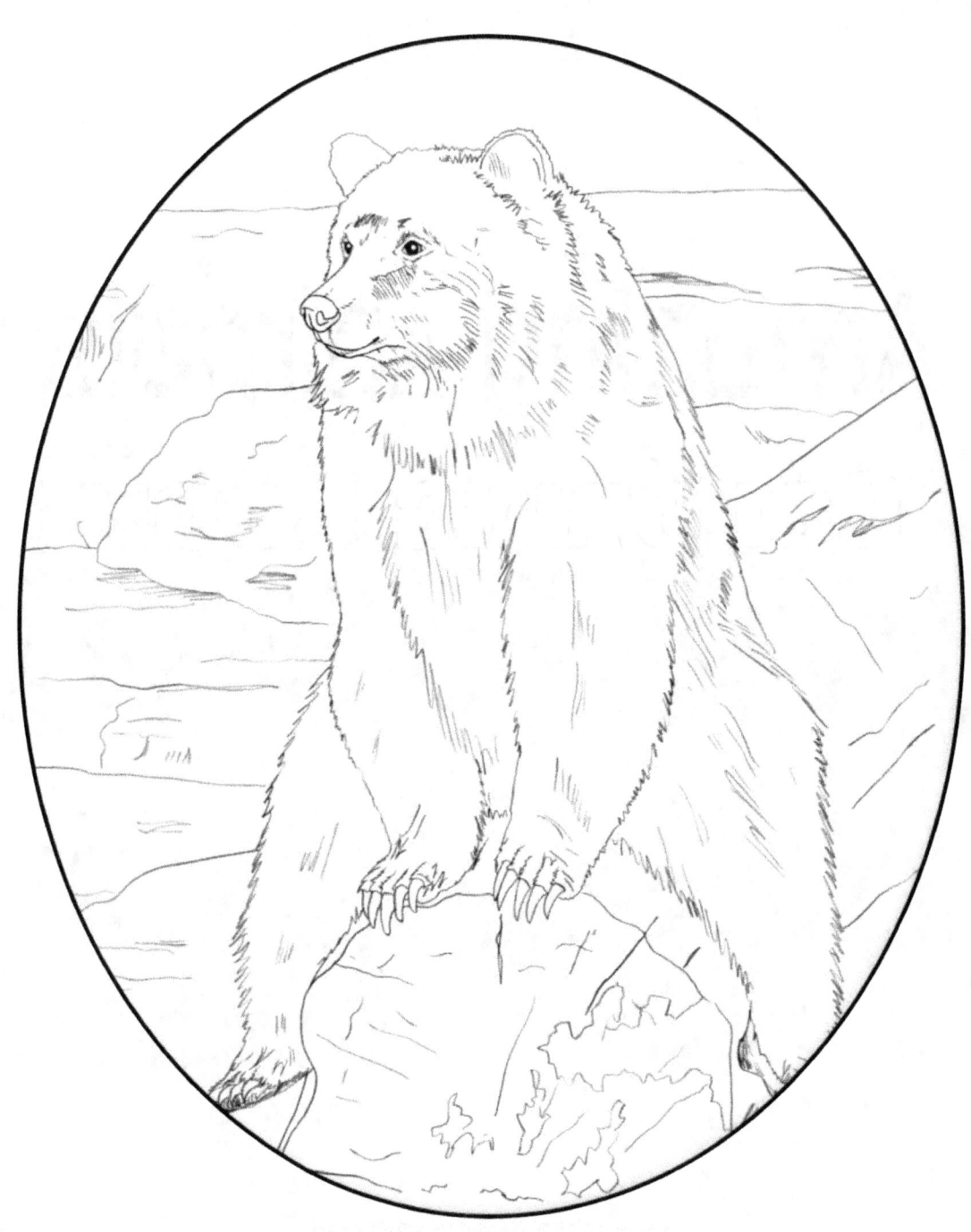

Amazing Animals
COLORING BOOK

Drawings by

ROBERT A. POWELL

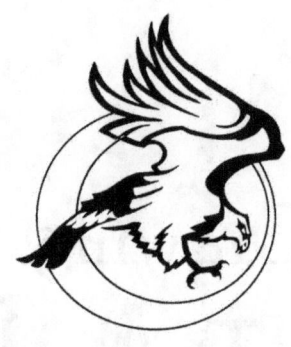

www.kyhawke.com

Published & Distributed by:

SilverHawke Publications

Danville, Kentucky 40423

ISBN 978-1543295795

Welcome

Amazing Animals Coloring Book offers a collection of sketches by Artist Robert A. Powell of animals you might encounter during an adventure at the Zoo. When you visit the Zoo you are able to meet different birds, mammals and reptiles first-hand.

When you sit down with this coloring book, you can refresh that experience and gain a new understanding of each one from your memory, and others you may have missed. This is an opportunity to capture them as a lasting art piece or to simply enhance the experience with a camouflage of your own choosing.

This book includes a variety of subjects that should spark the artistic interest of nearly any age. The author-artist has written a brief description about each animal depicted. This volume will become a treasured portfolio of your adventure with the animals.

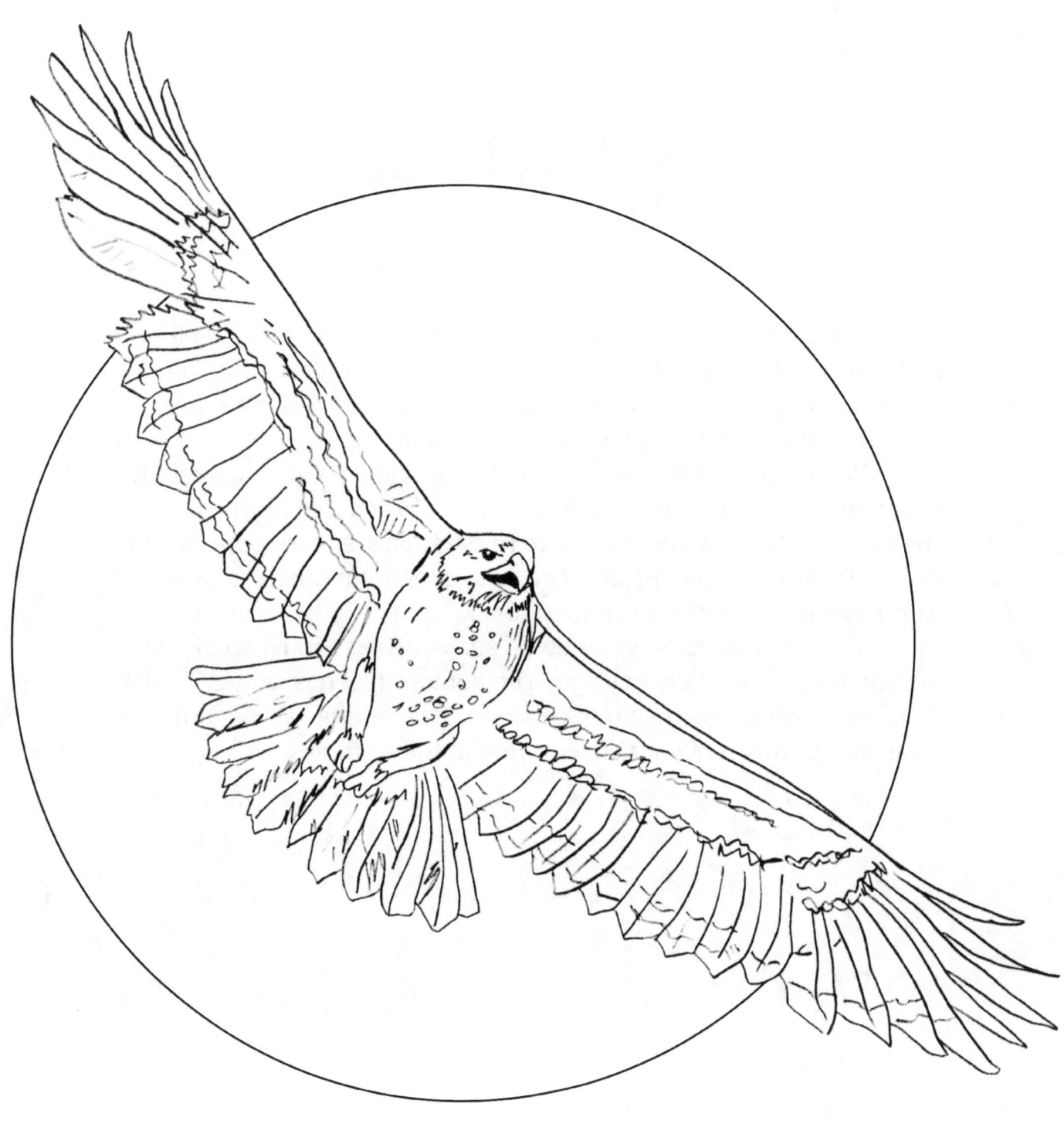

Table of Contents

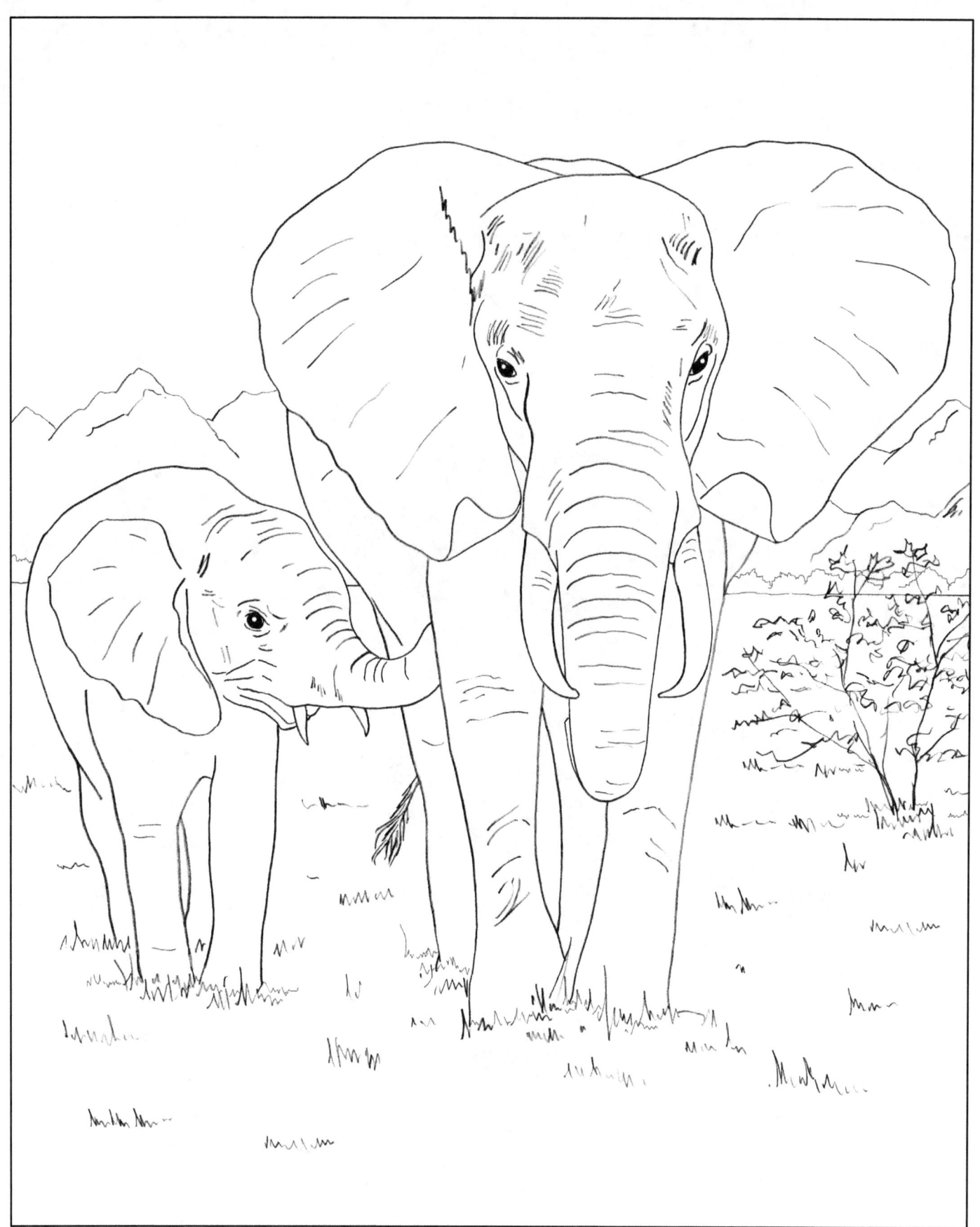

Elephant
African Elephant from south of the Sahara Desert

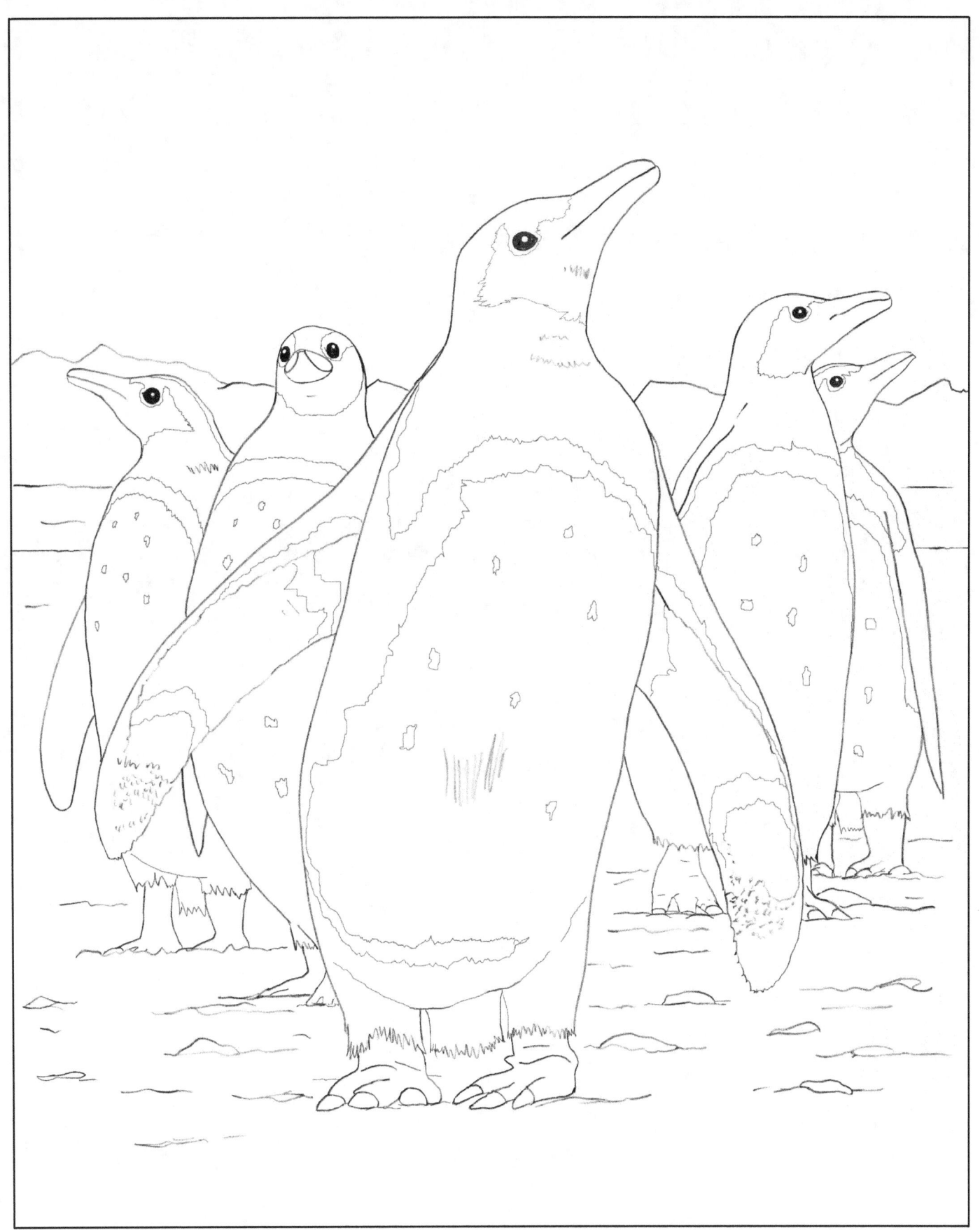

African Penguin
Also known as the jackass penguin

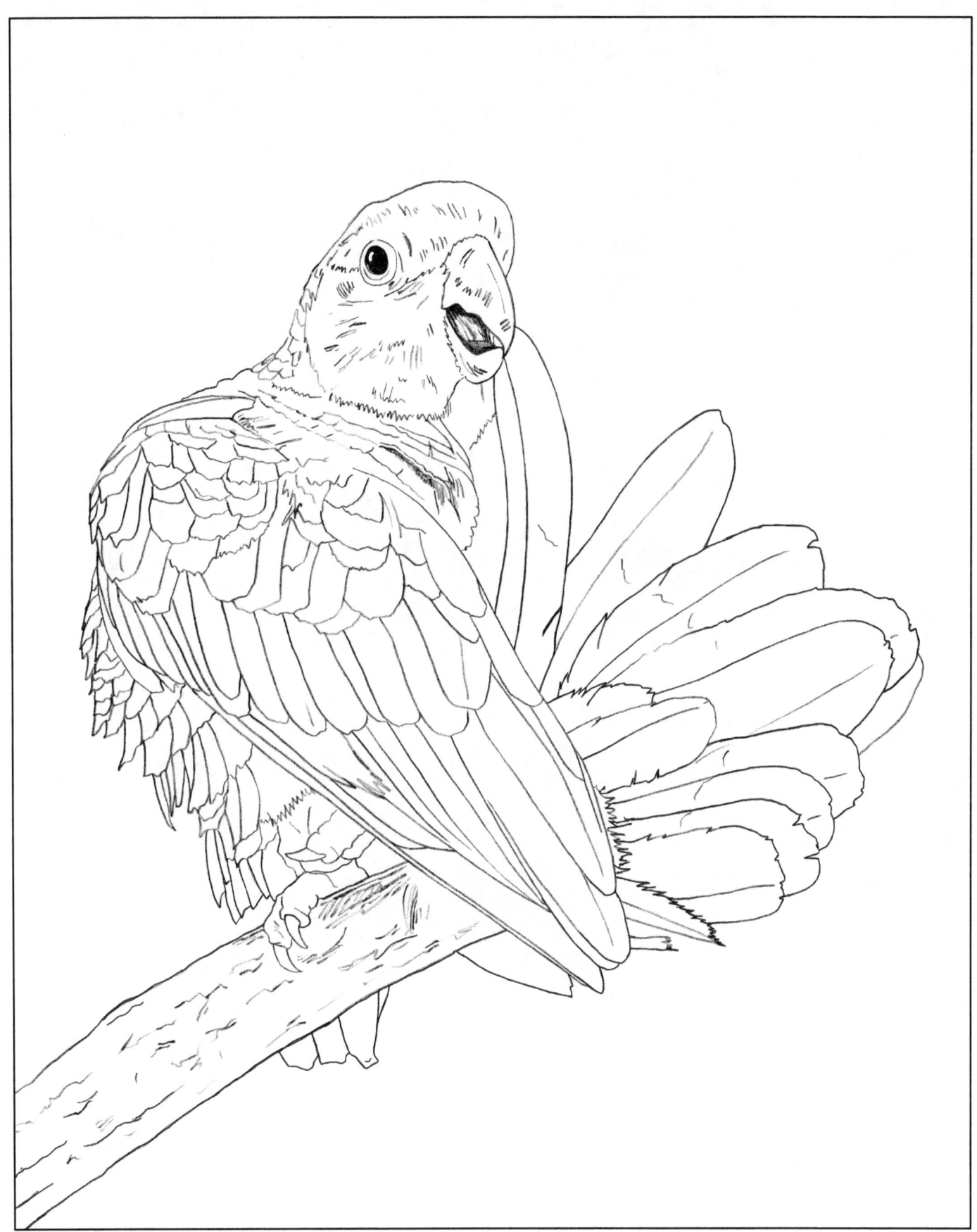

Amazon Parrot
Yellow-Headed Amazon Parrot from the Caribbean

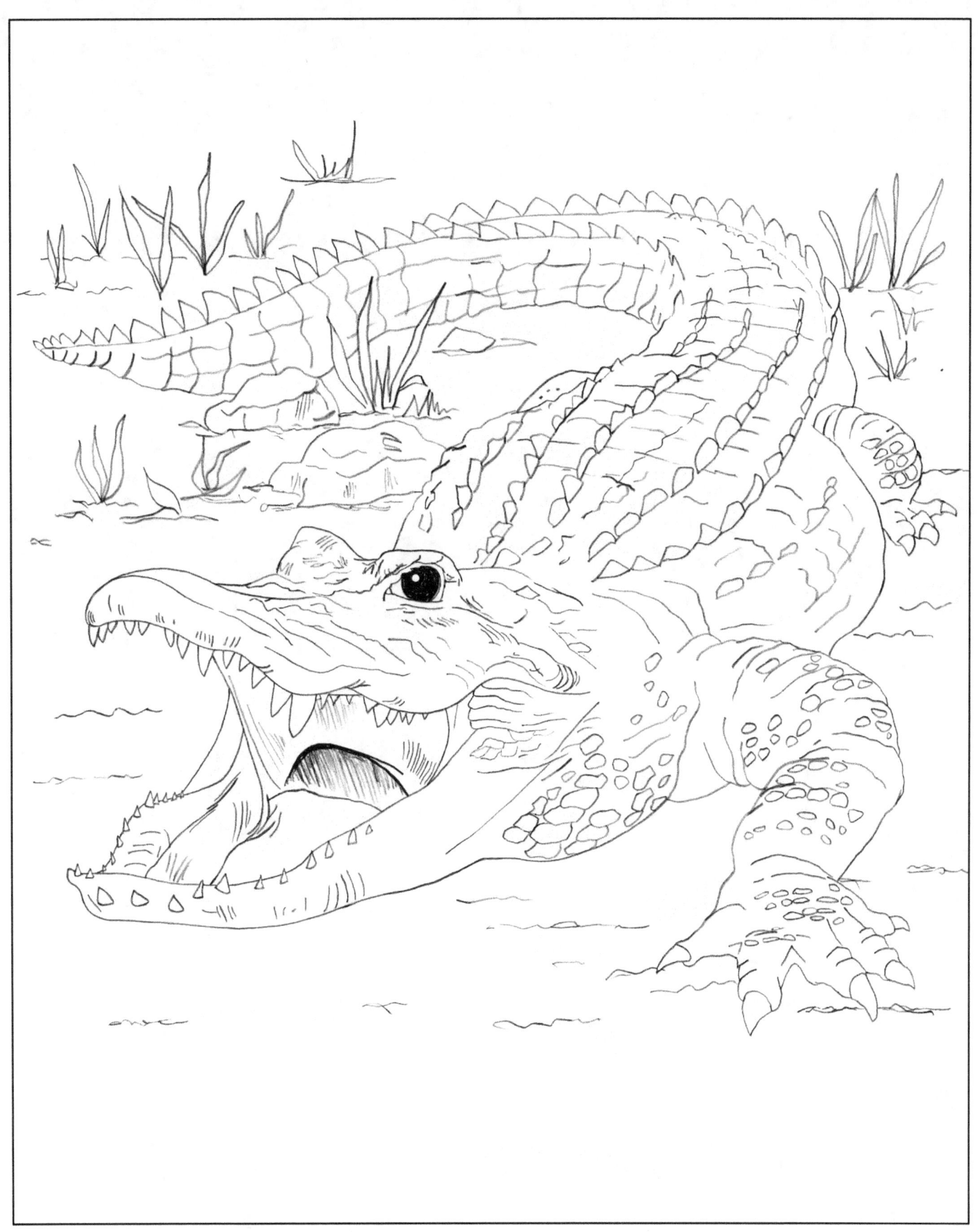

American Alligator

American alligator from freshwater wetlands

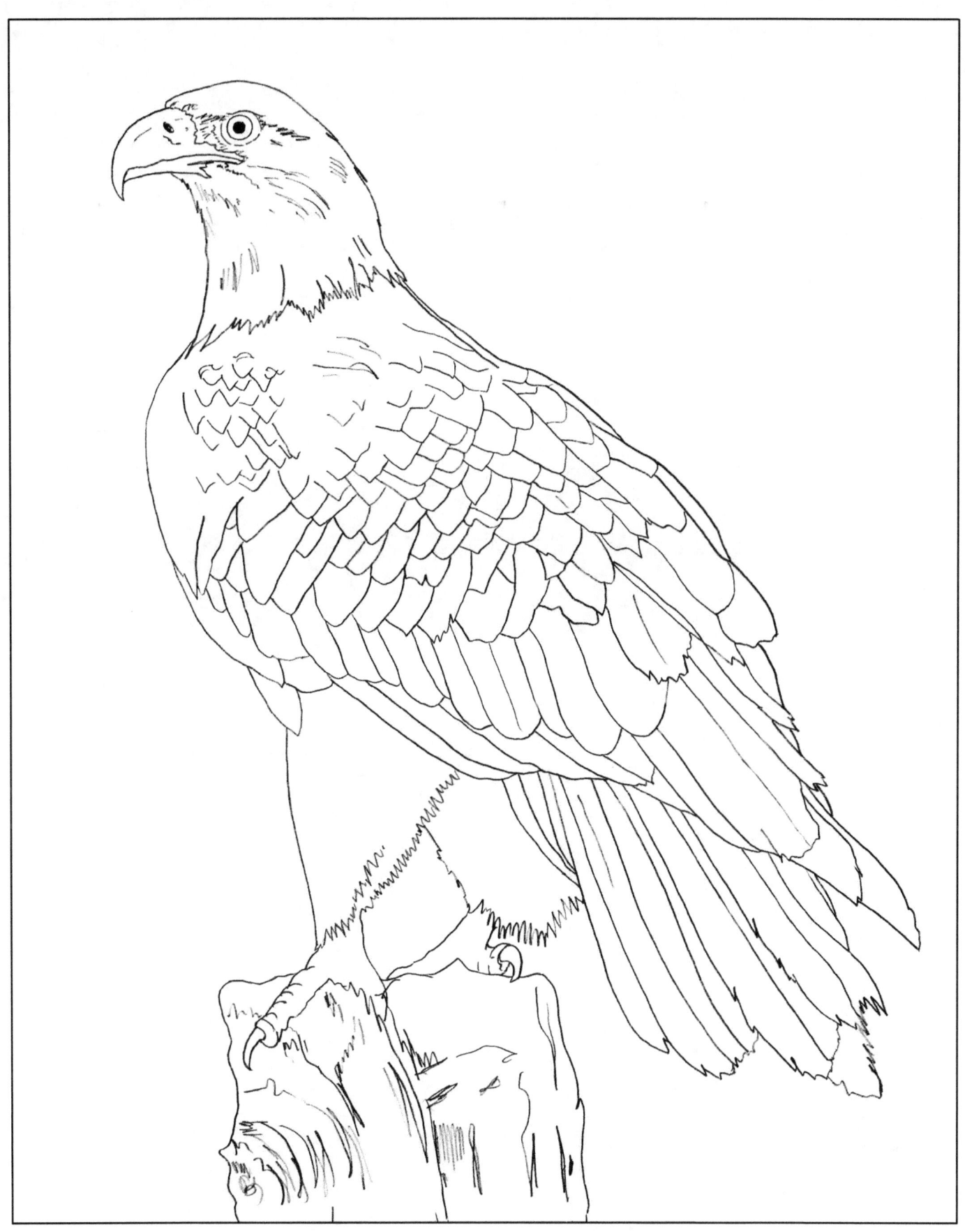

Bald Eagle
National bird of the United States of America

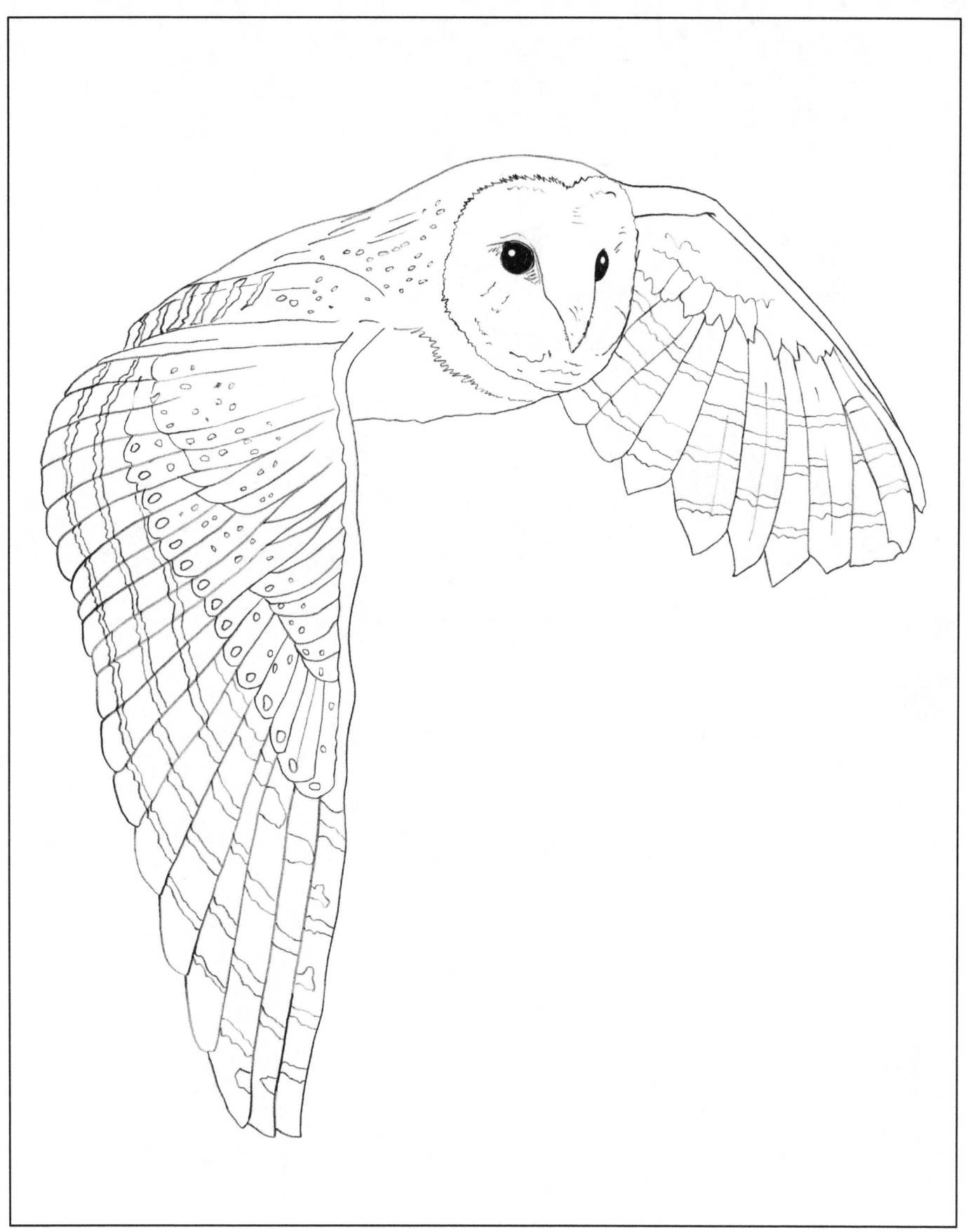

Barn Owl
Found in farm areas all over the world

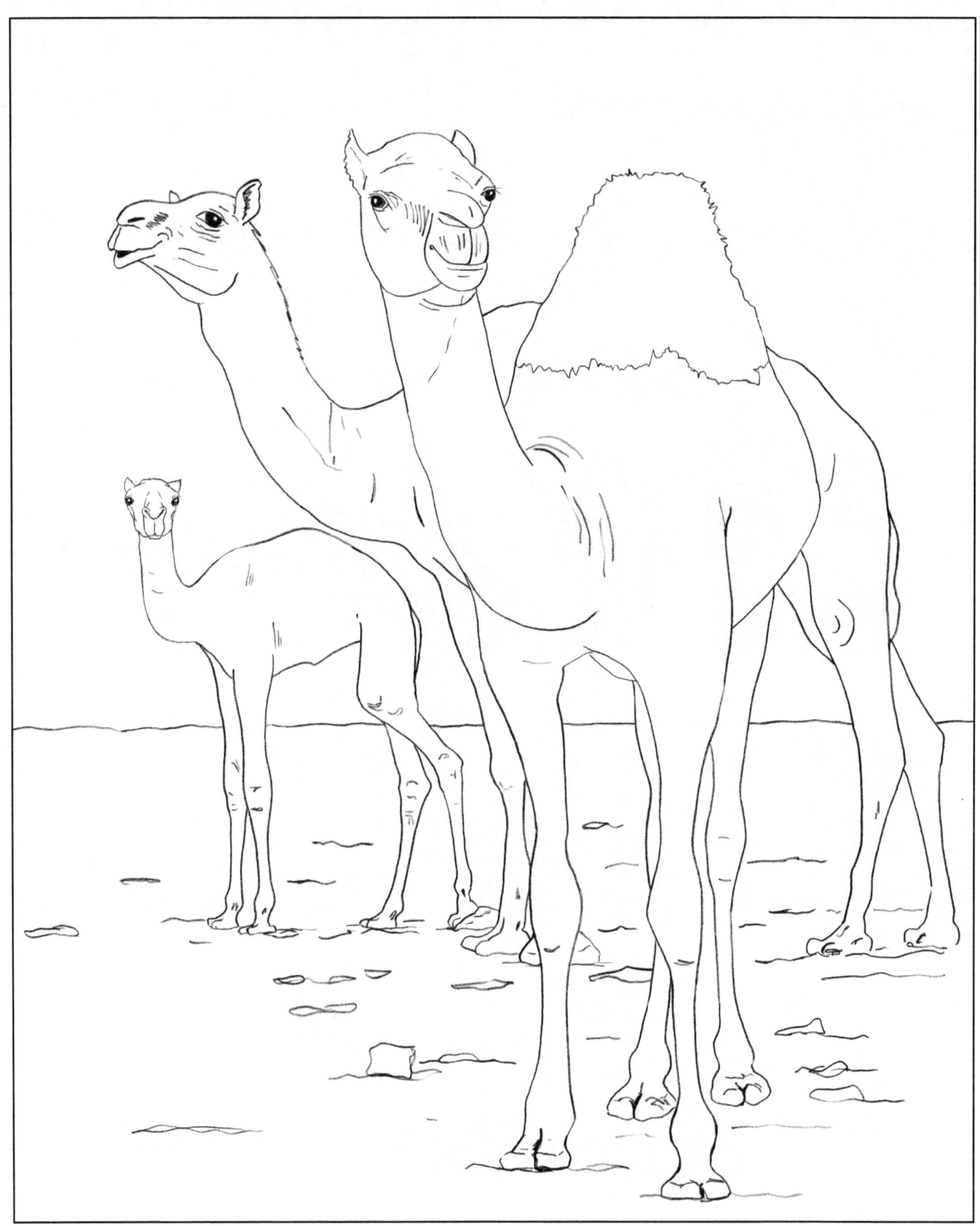

Dromedary Camel
Native to Southwest Asia and North Africa

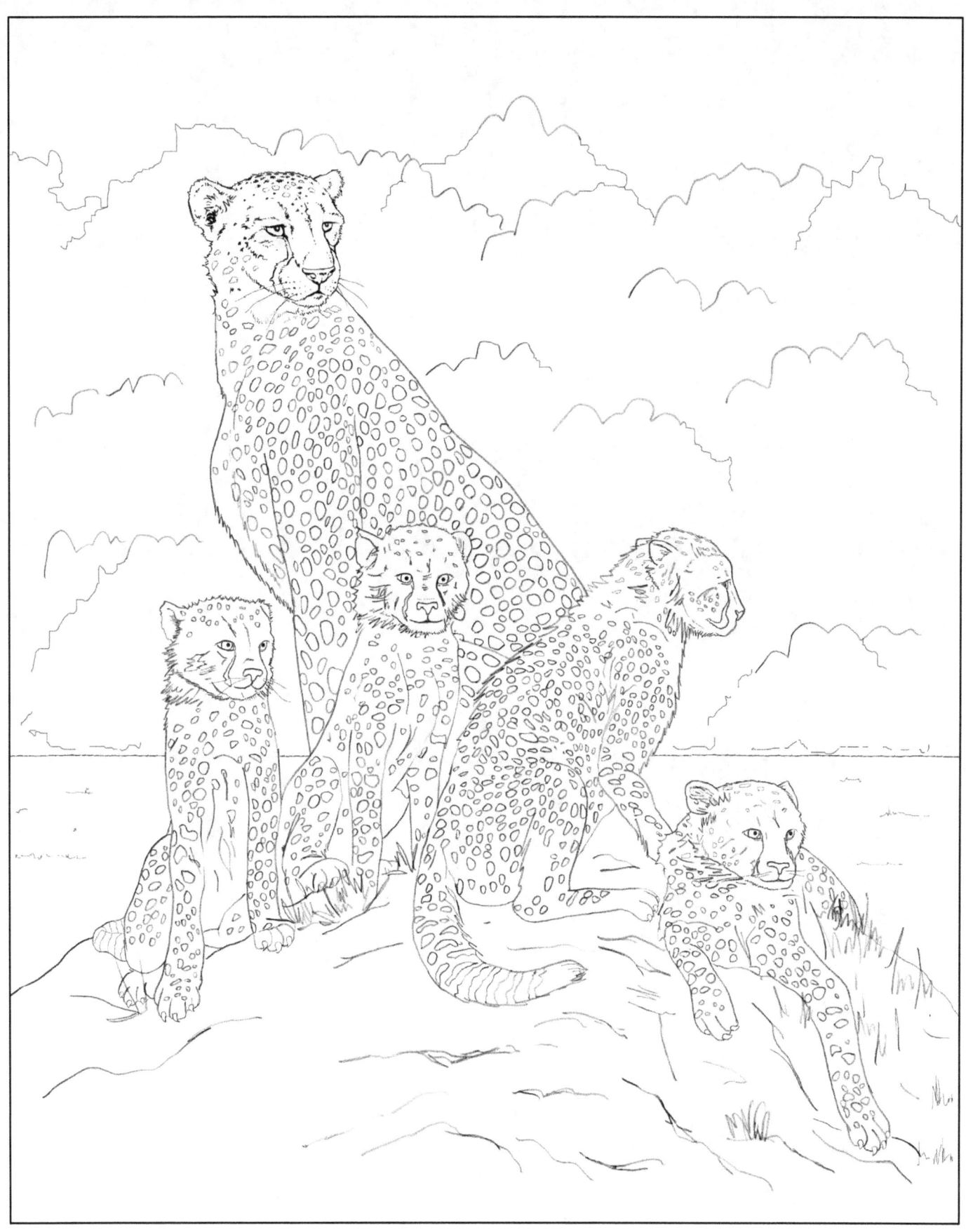

Cheetah

Cheetah mother and four cubs from Africa

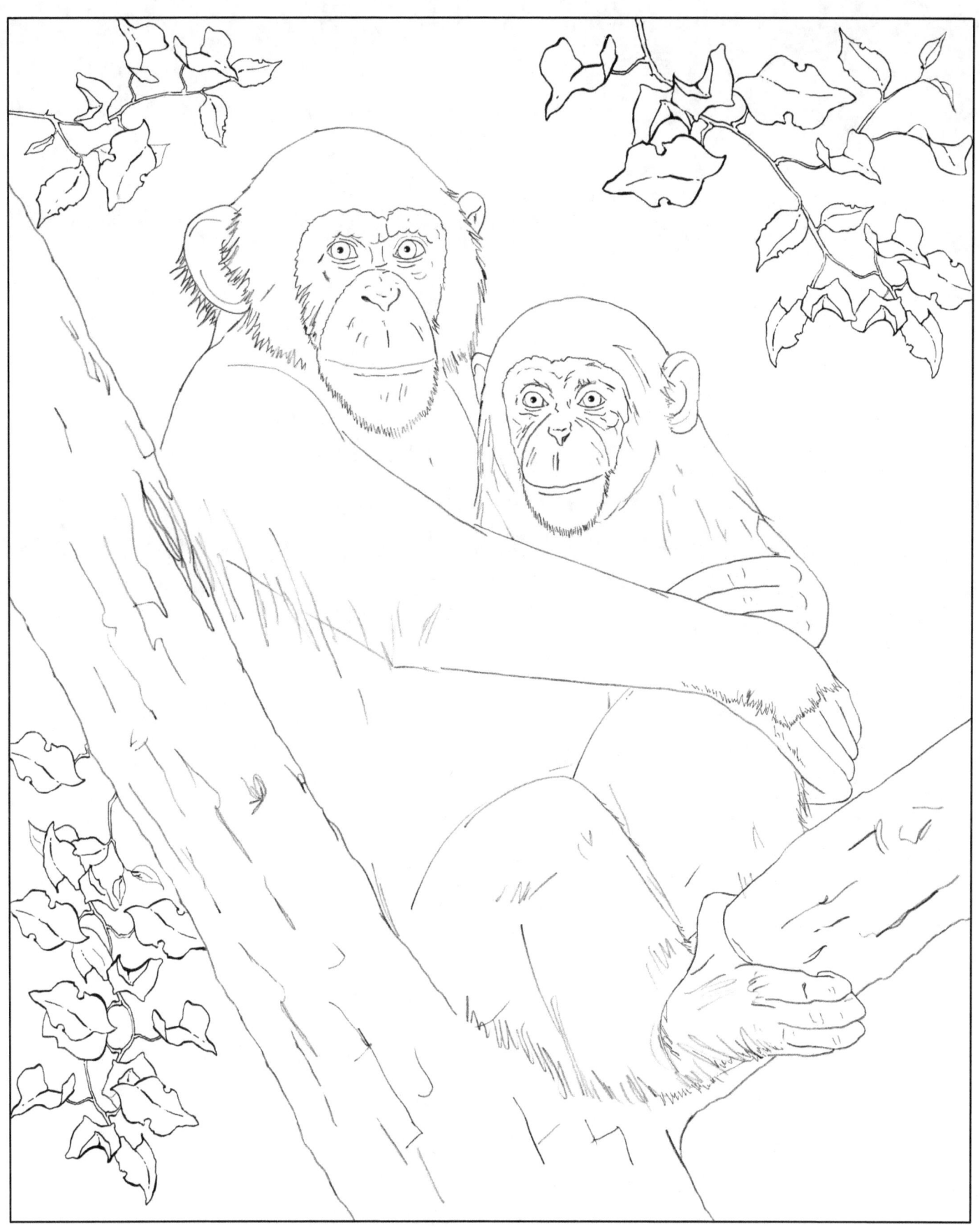

Chimpanzee
Part of the Great Ape family from the Congo

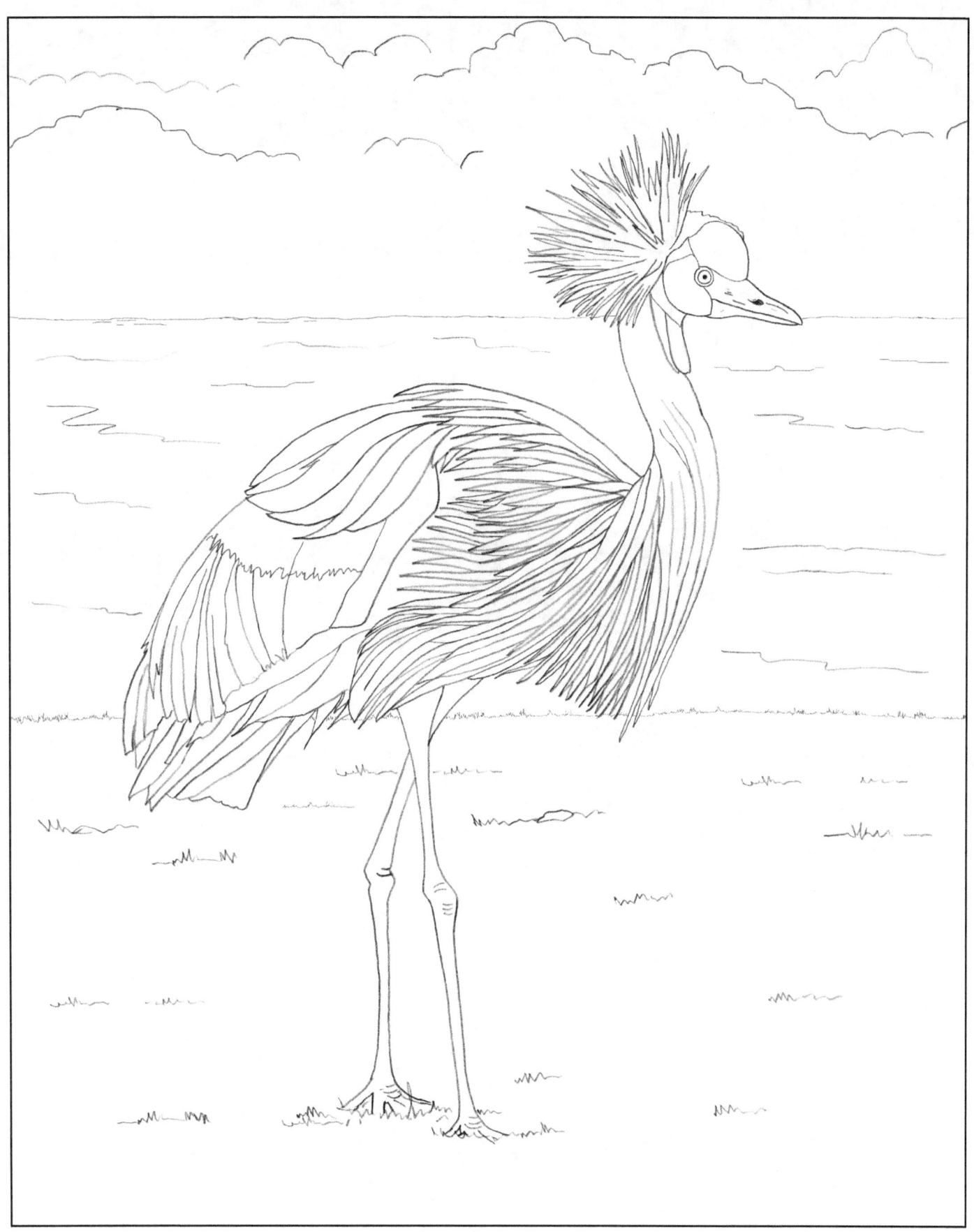

East African Crowned Crane

From dry savannah in Africa south of the Sahara Desert

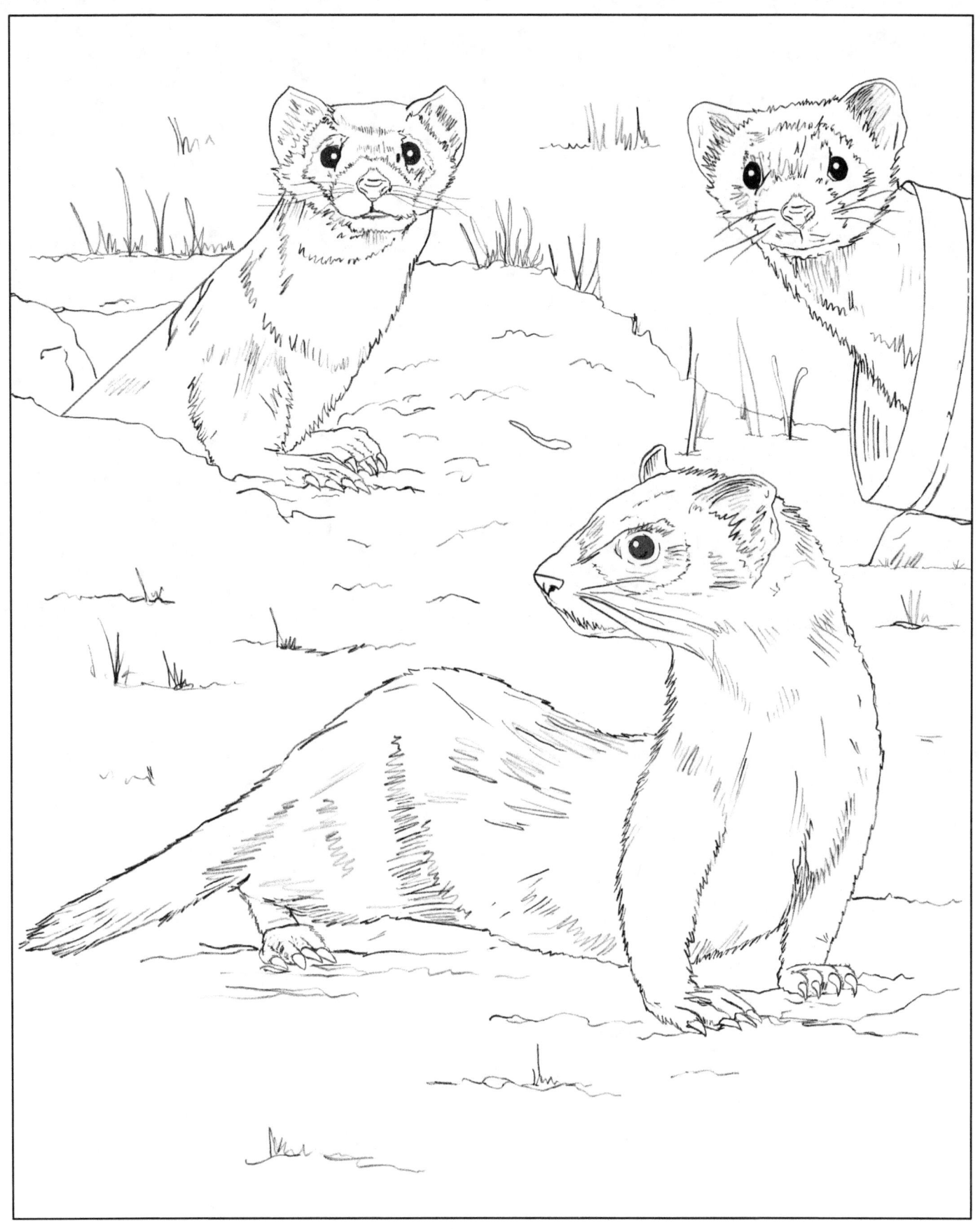

Black-footed Ferret
One of the most endangered mammals in North America

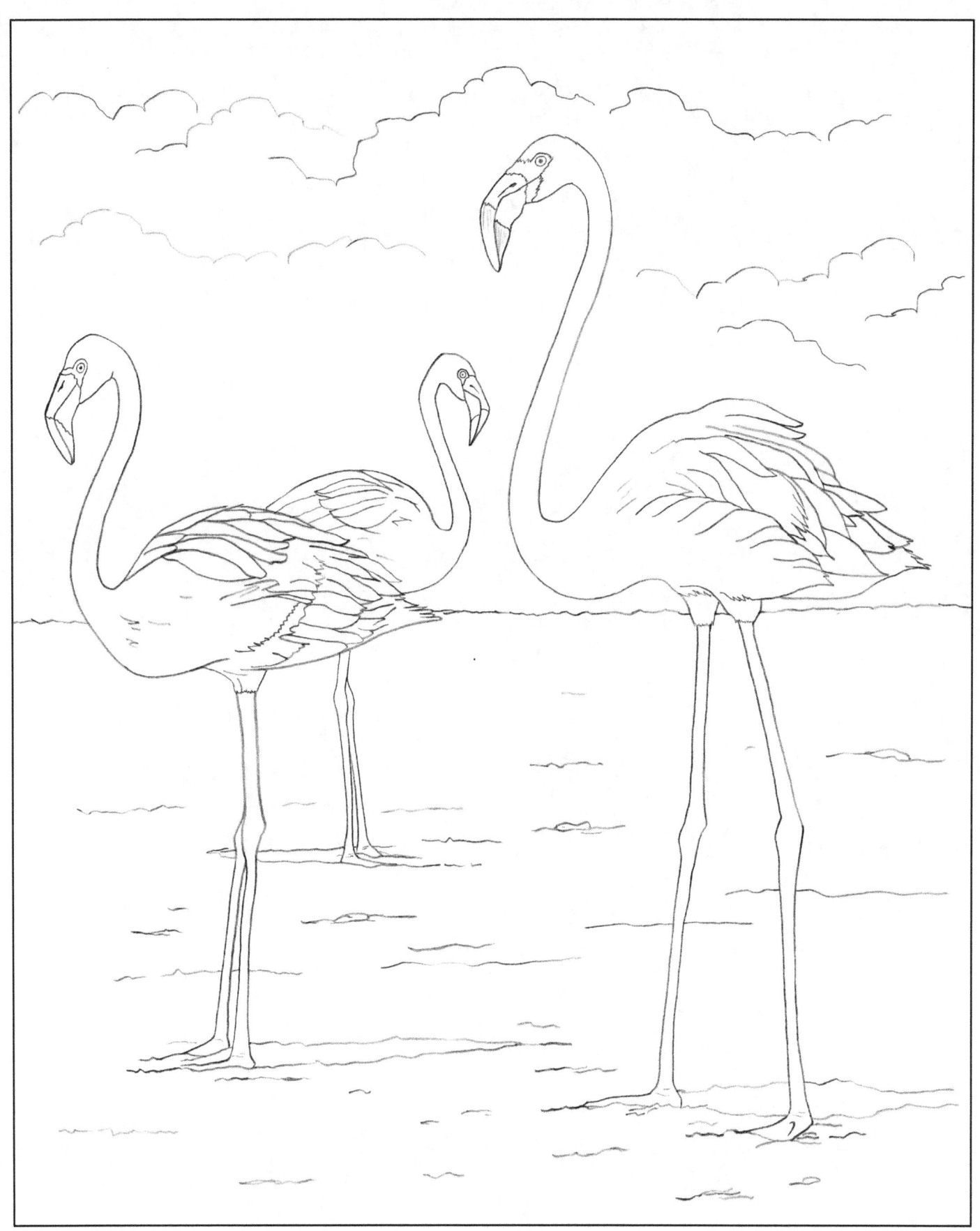

Flamingo
Greater Flamingo originally from Africa and Asia

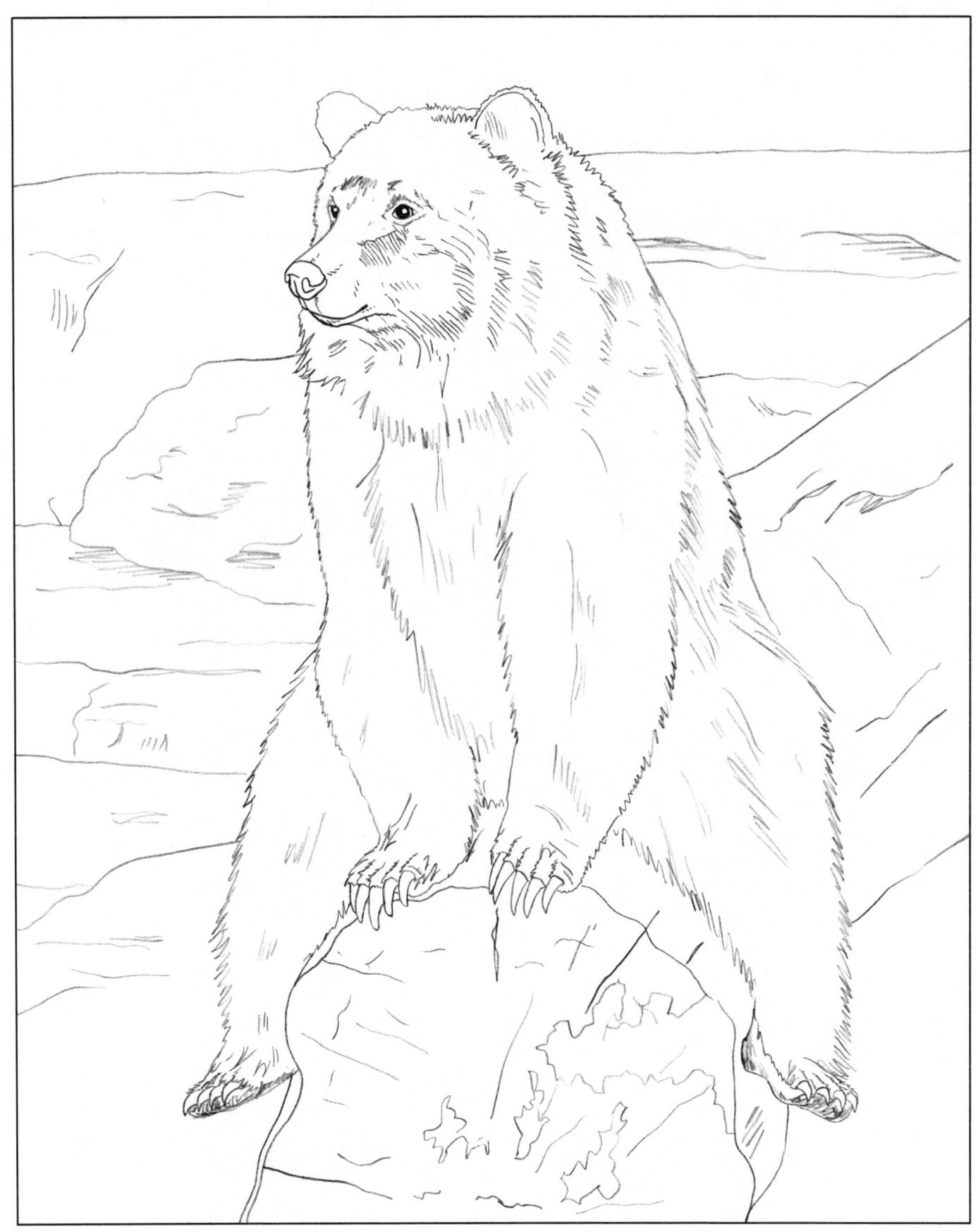

Florida Black Bear

This Florida Native is right at home

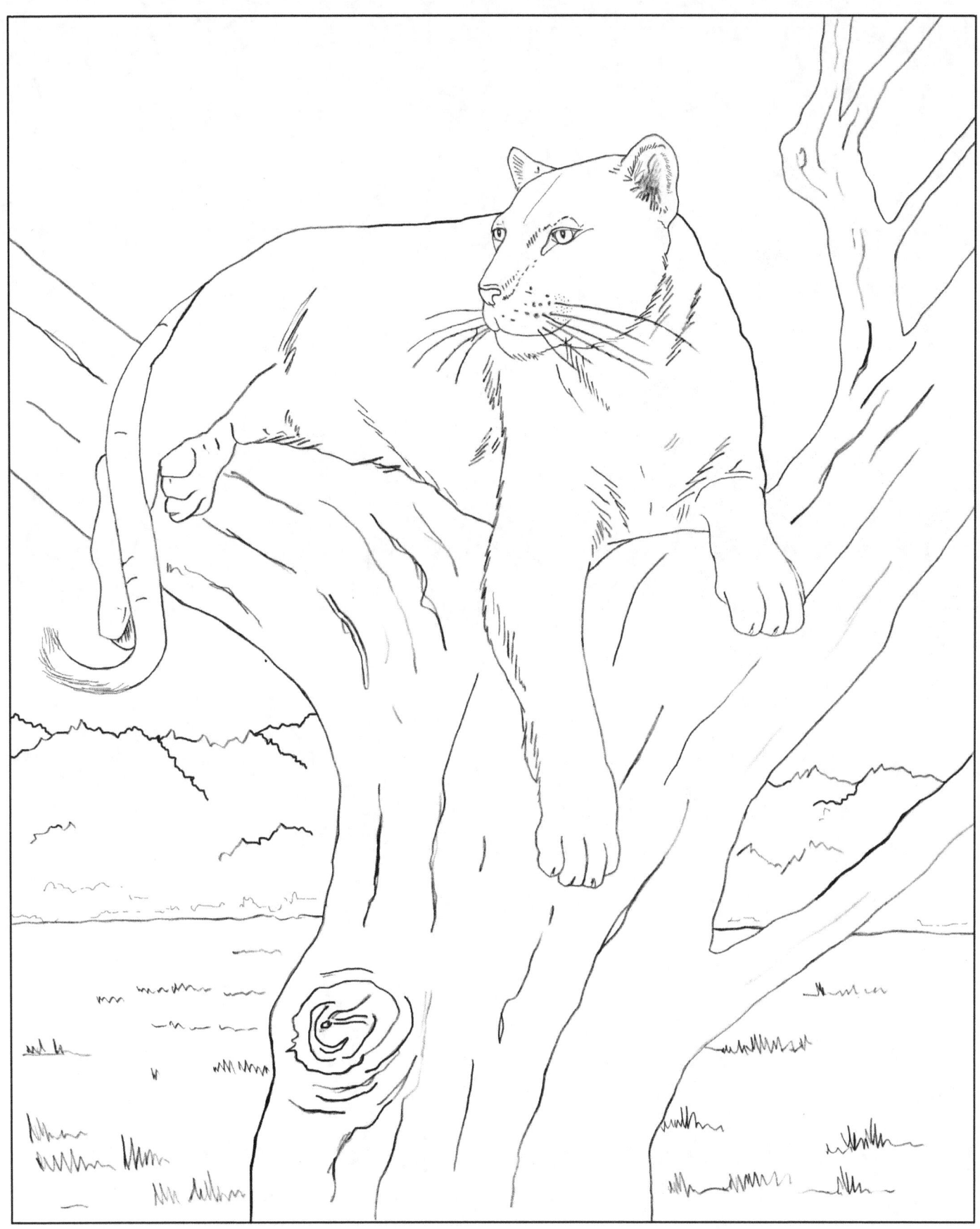

Florida Panther

This member of the cougar family is the State Animal of Florida

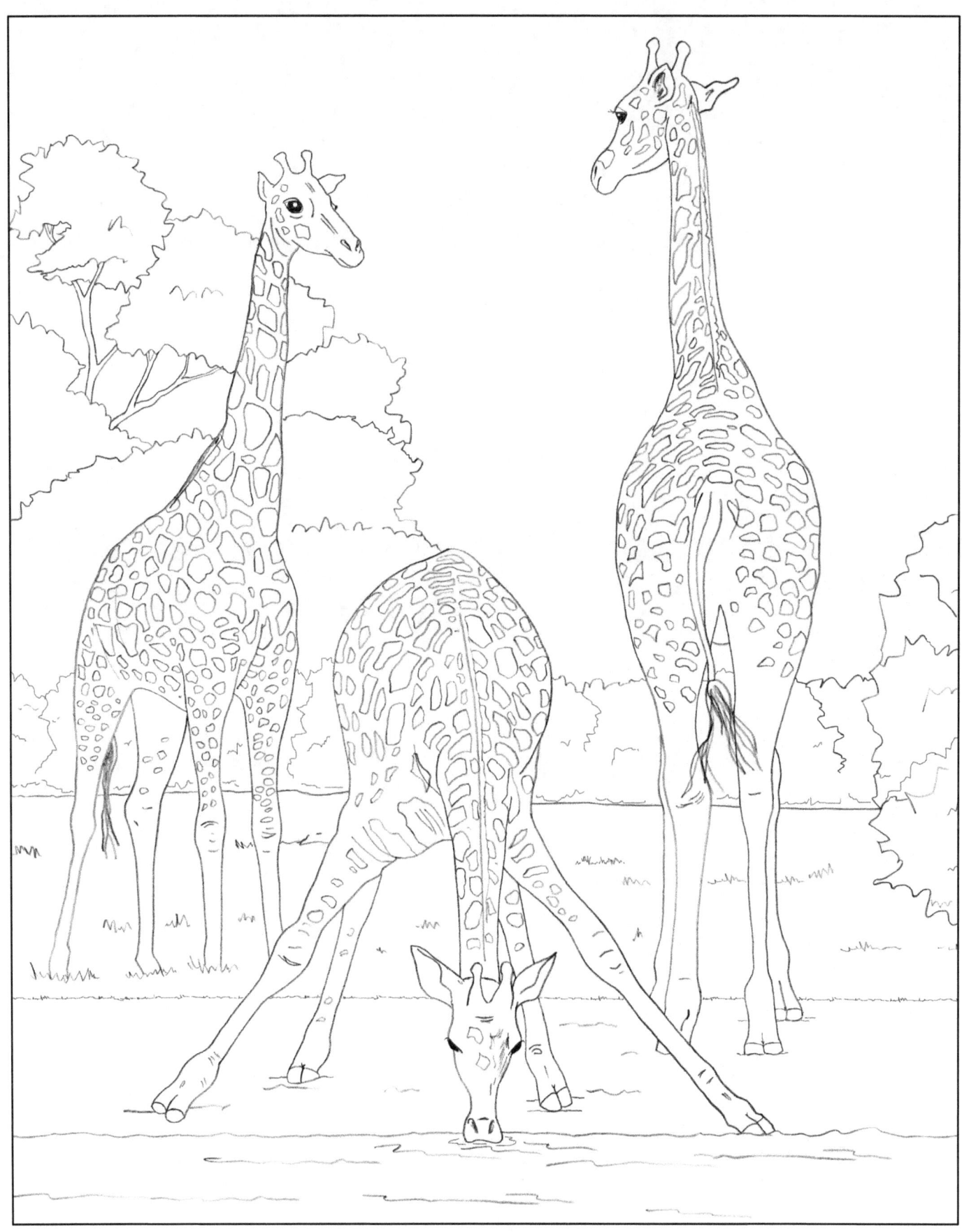

Giraffe
Masai giraffe is found primarily in Kenya and in Tanzania

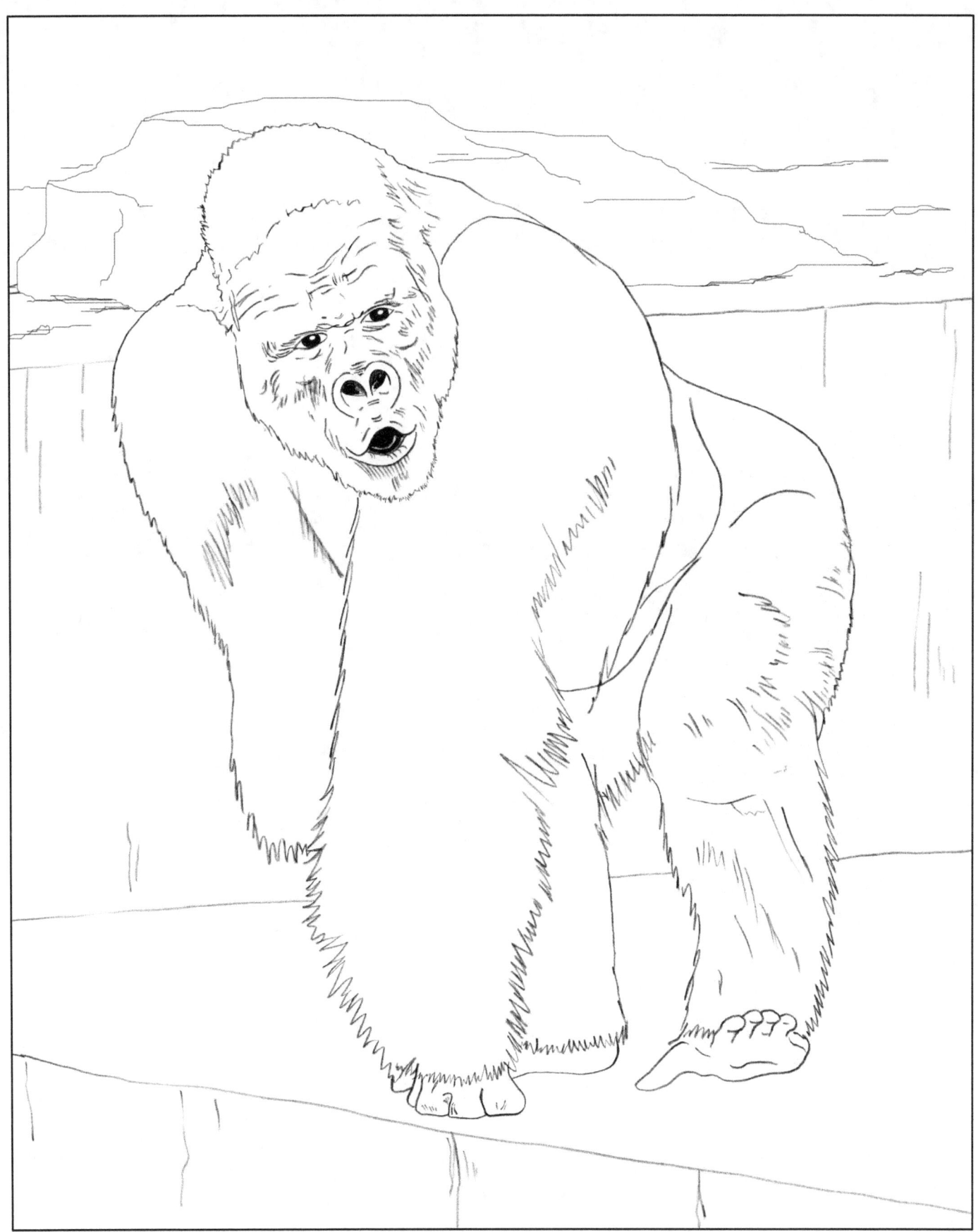

Gorilla
Western Lowland Gorilla from the Congo region of Africa

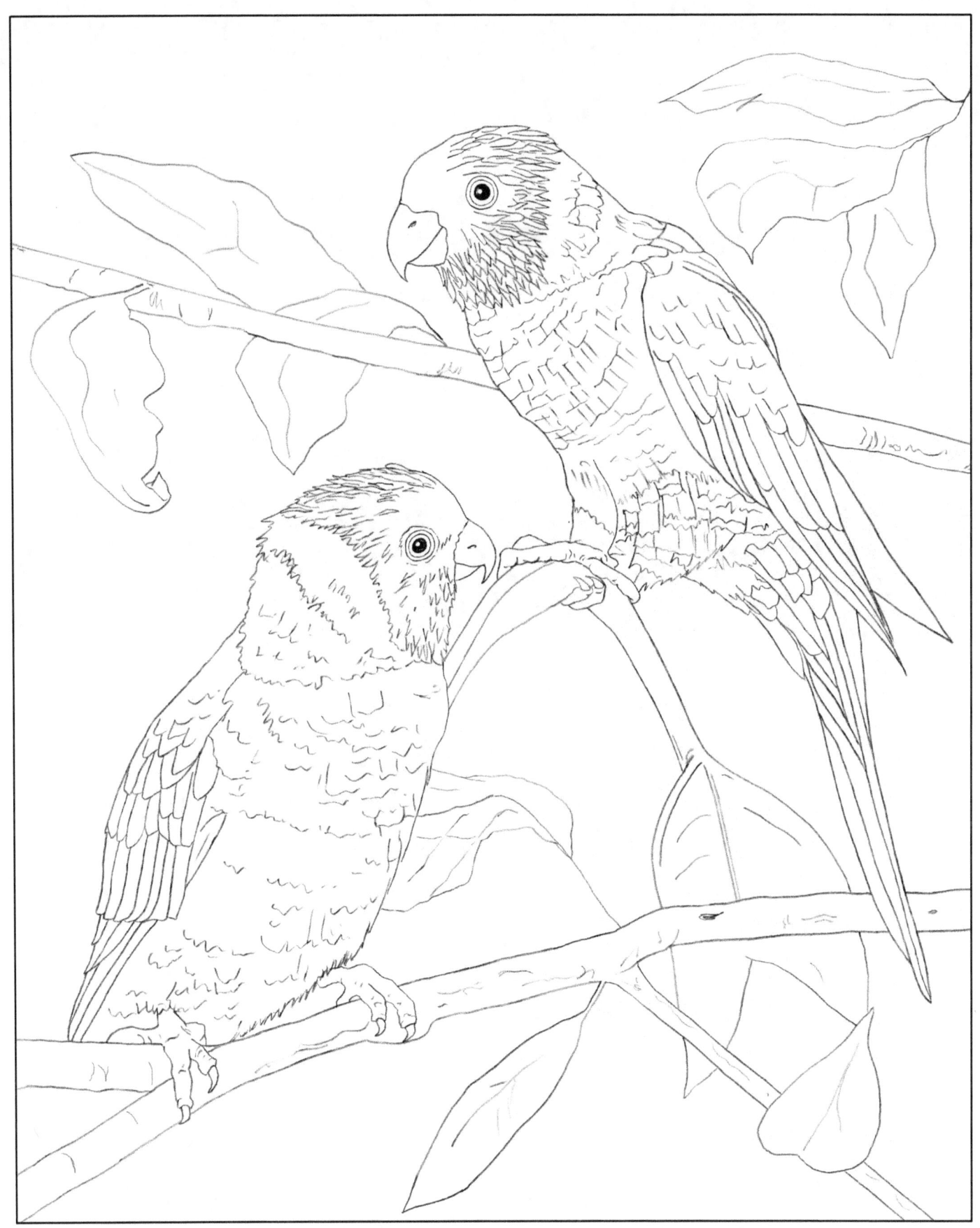

Green-napped Lorikeet
Most common of the colorful Rainbow Lorikeet parrots

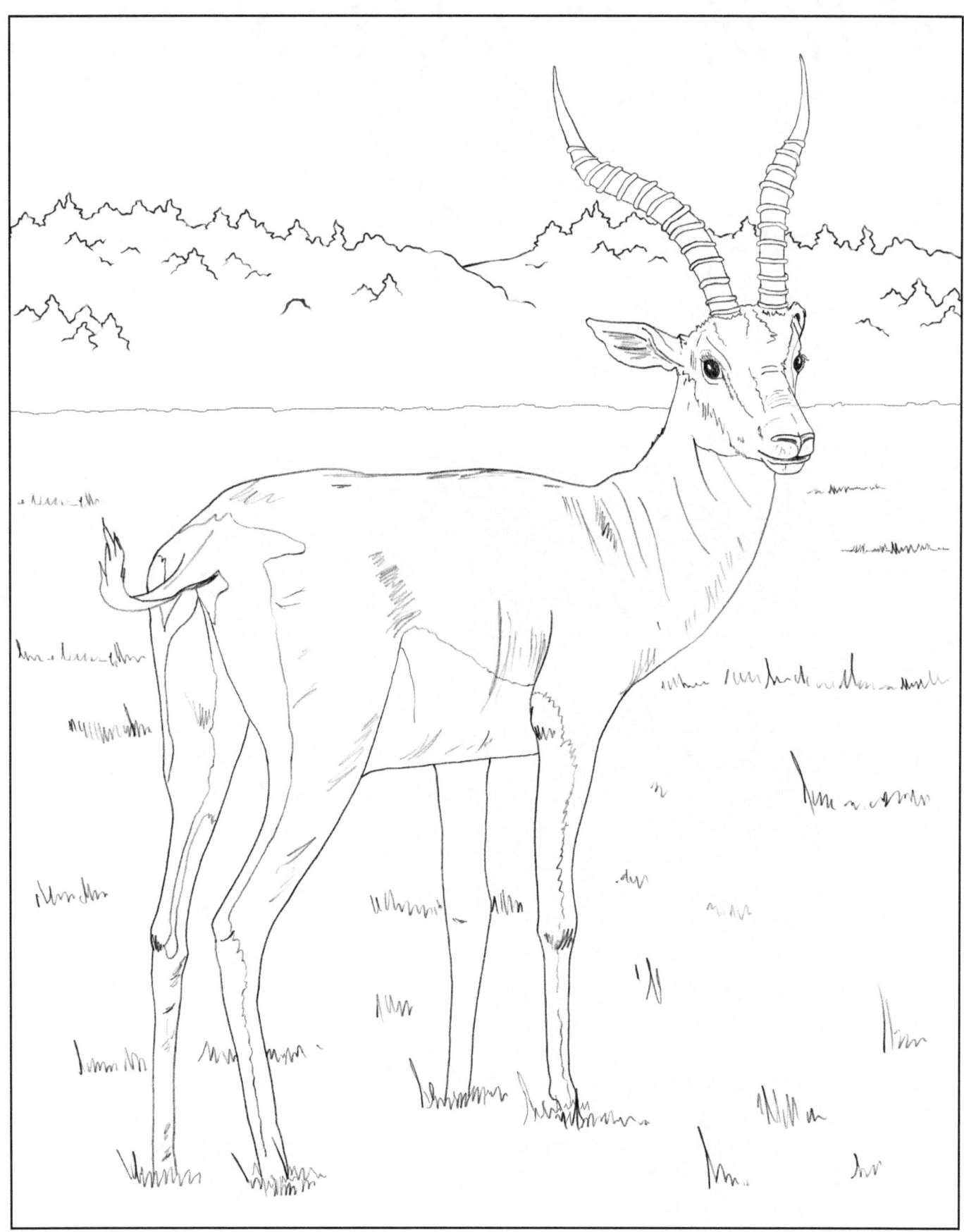

Impala
Kenya Impala from southern Africa

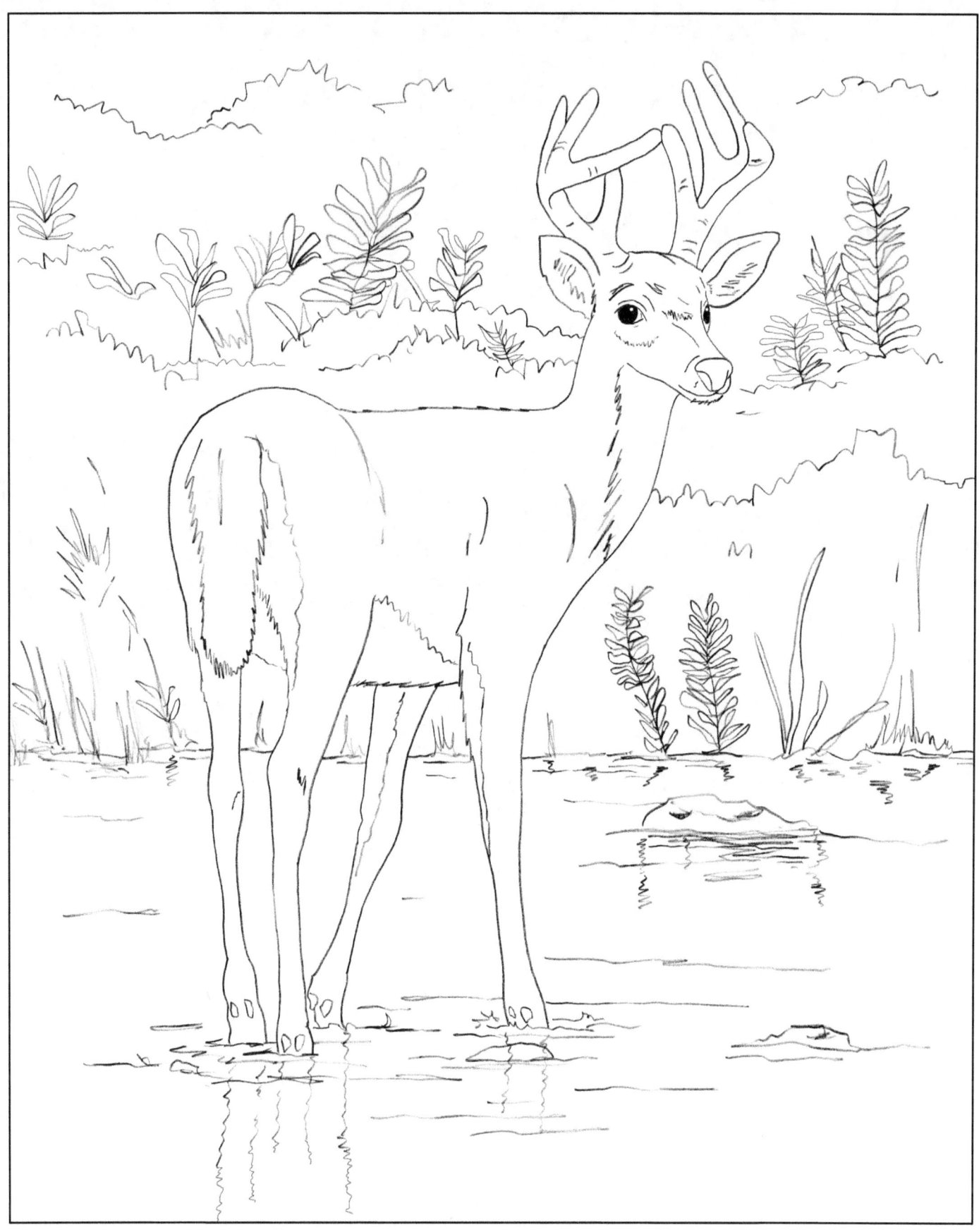

Key Deer

The smallest North American deer is unique to the Florida Keys

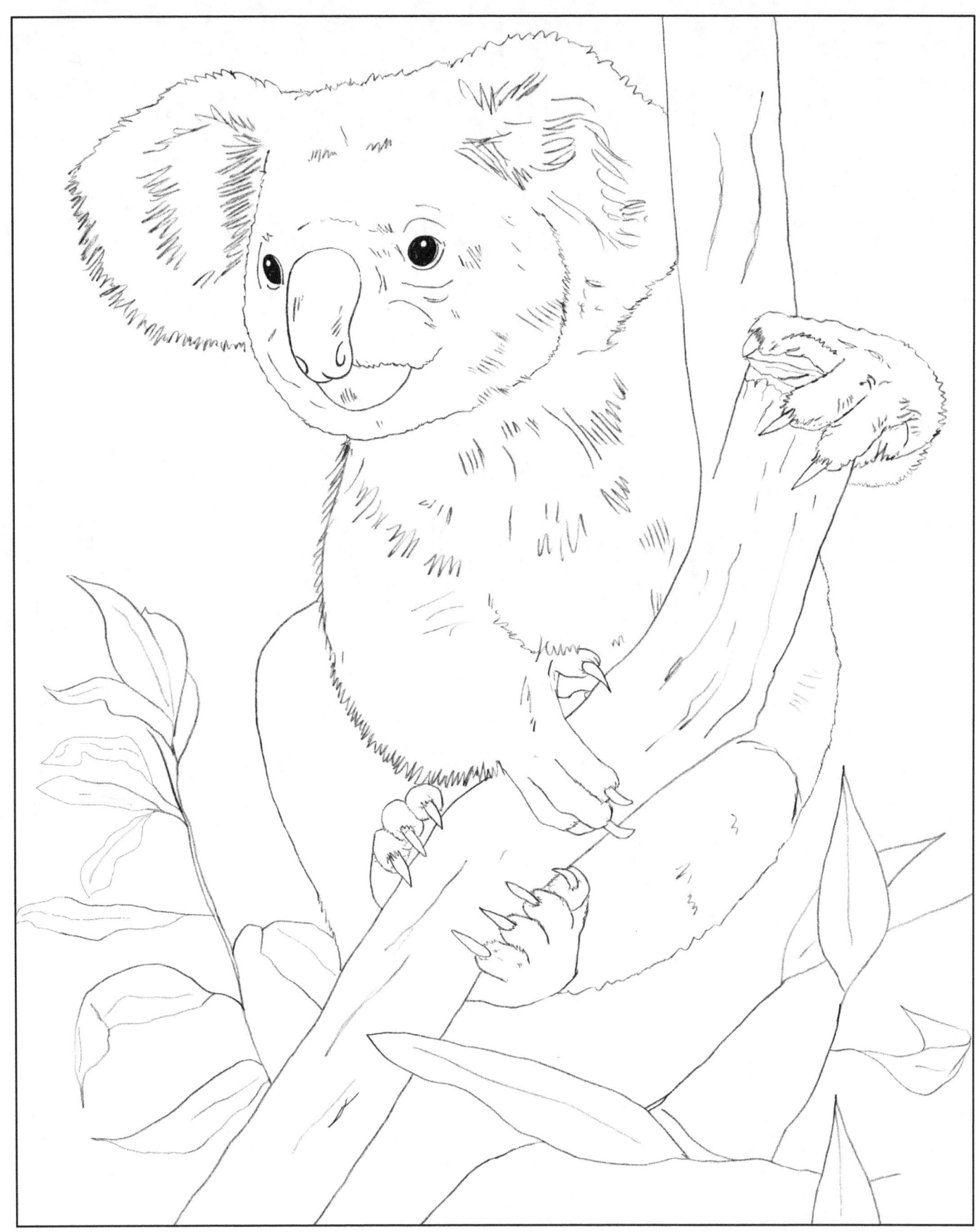

Koala
A herbivorous marsupial native to Australia

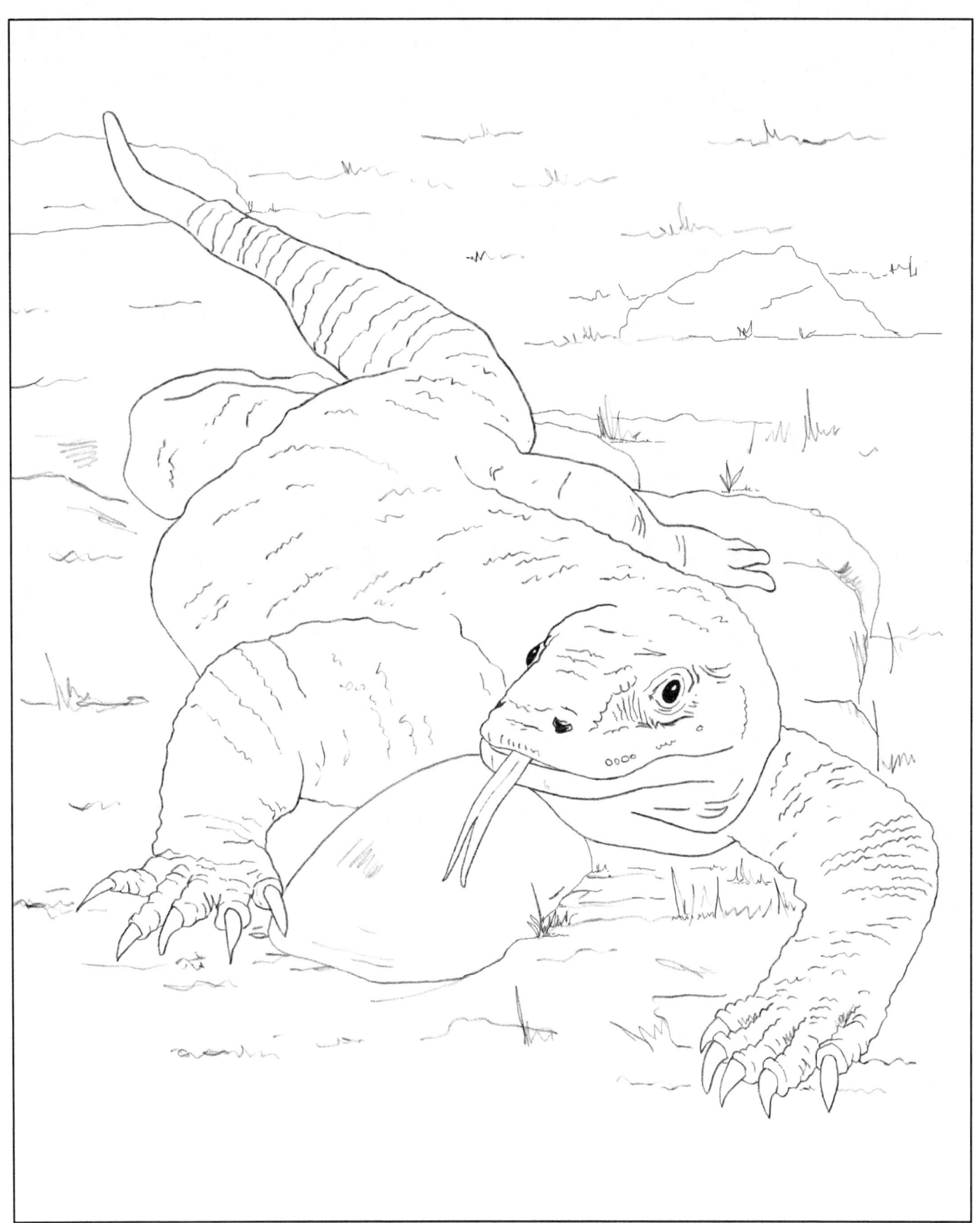

Komodo Dragon
Originally discovered on Komodo Island in Indonesia

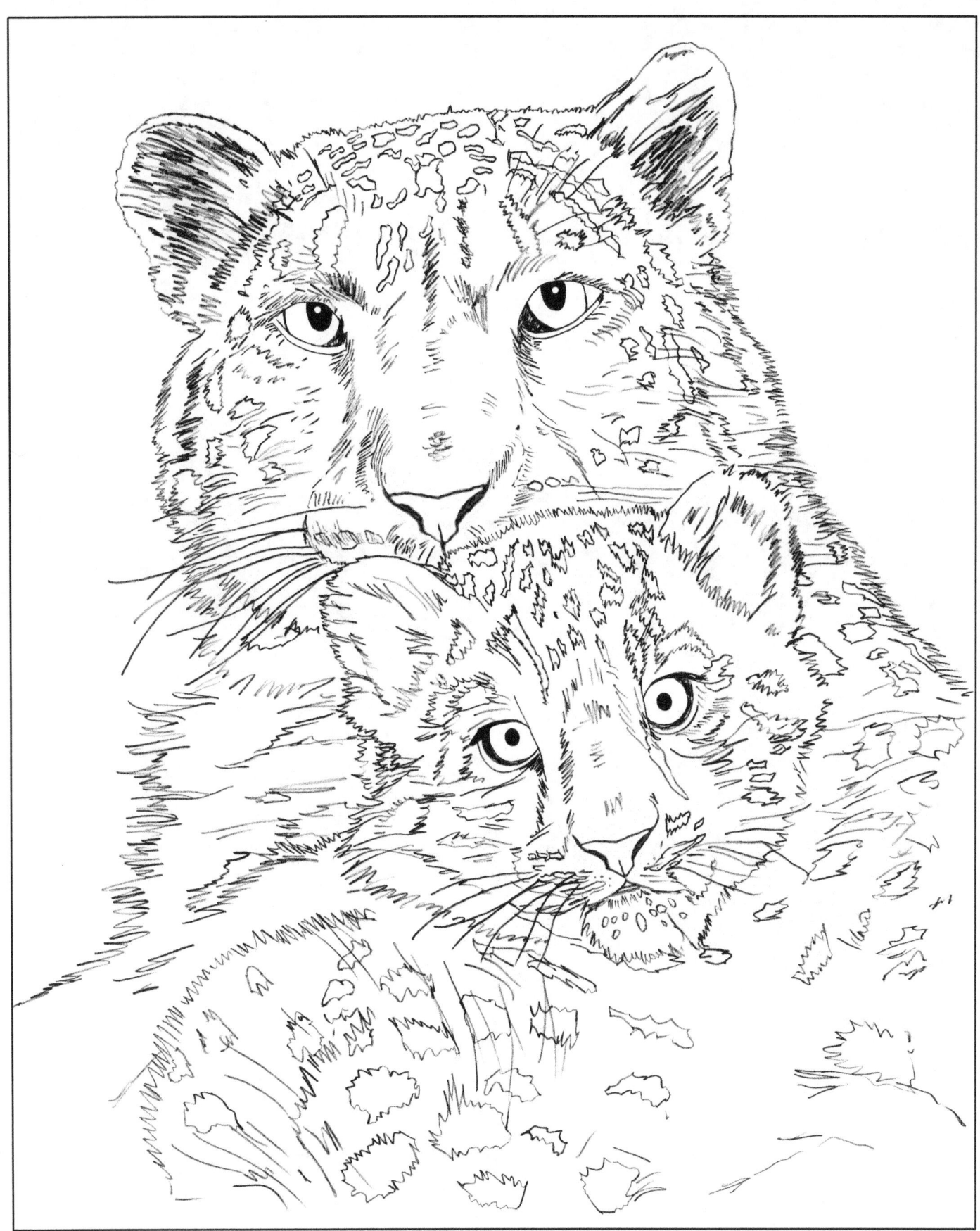

Leopard
From the Mountains of Central Asia

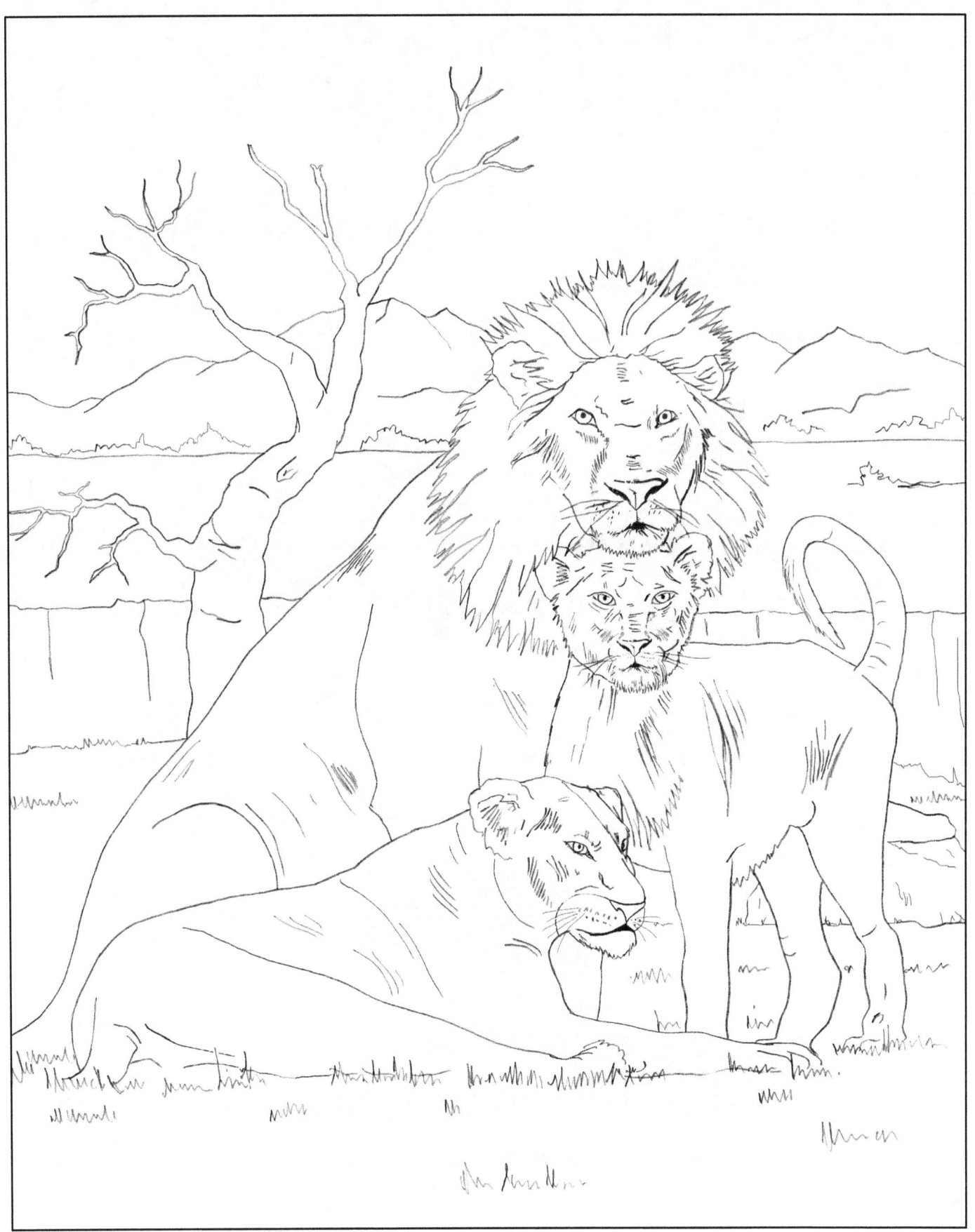

Lions
African Lions from southeastern Africa

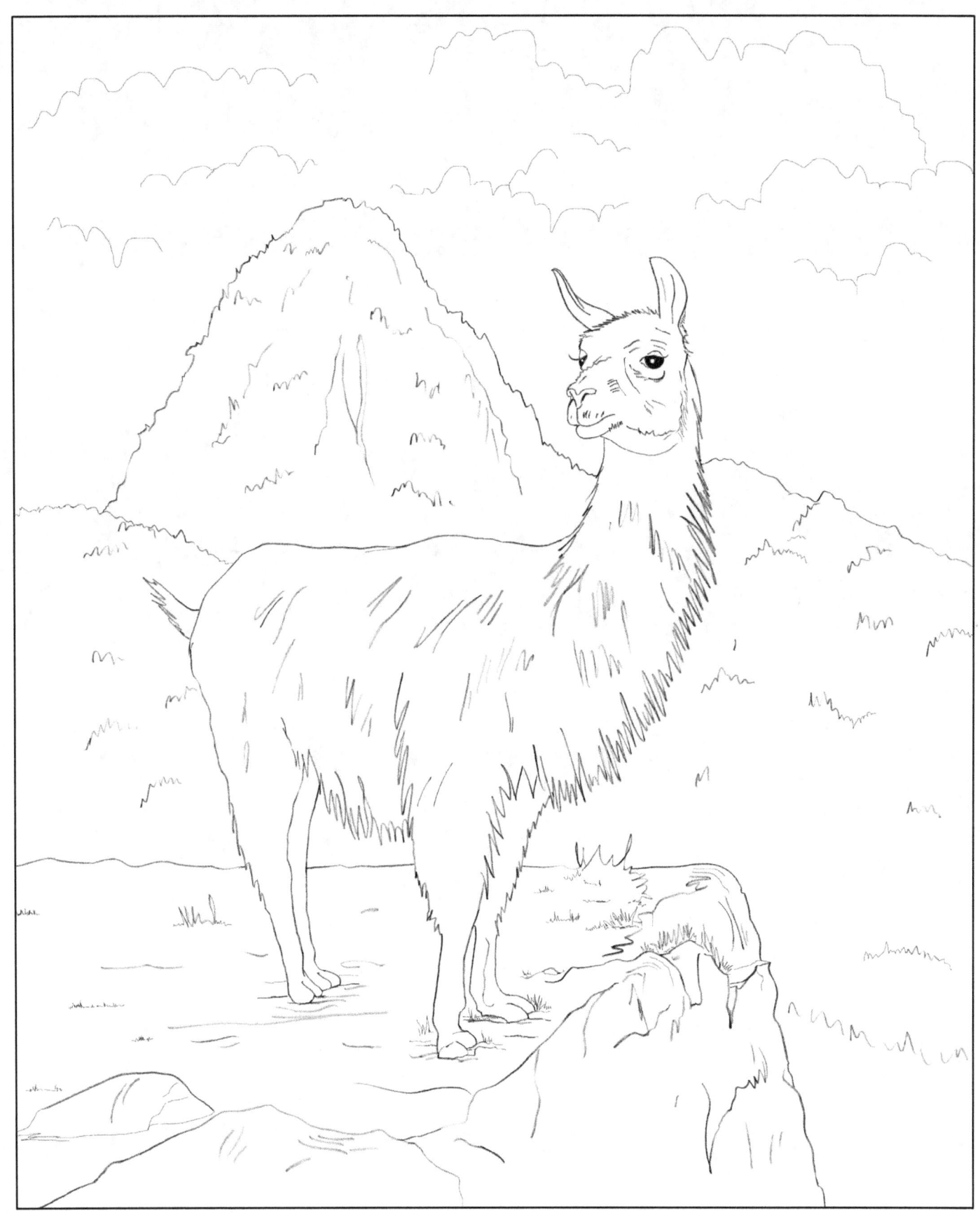

Llama
Domesticated South American camelid

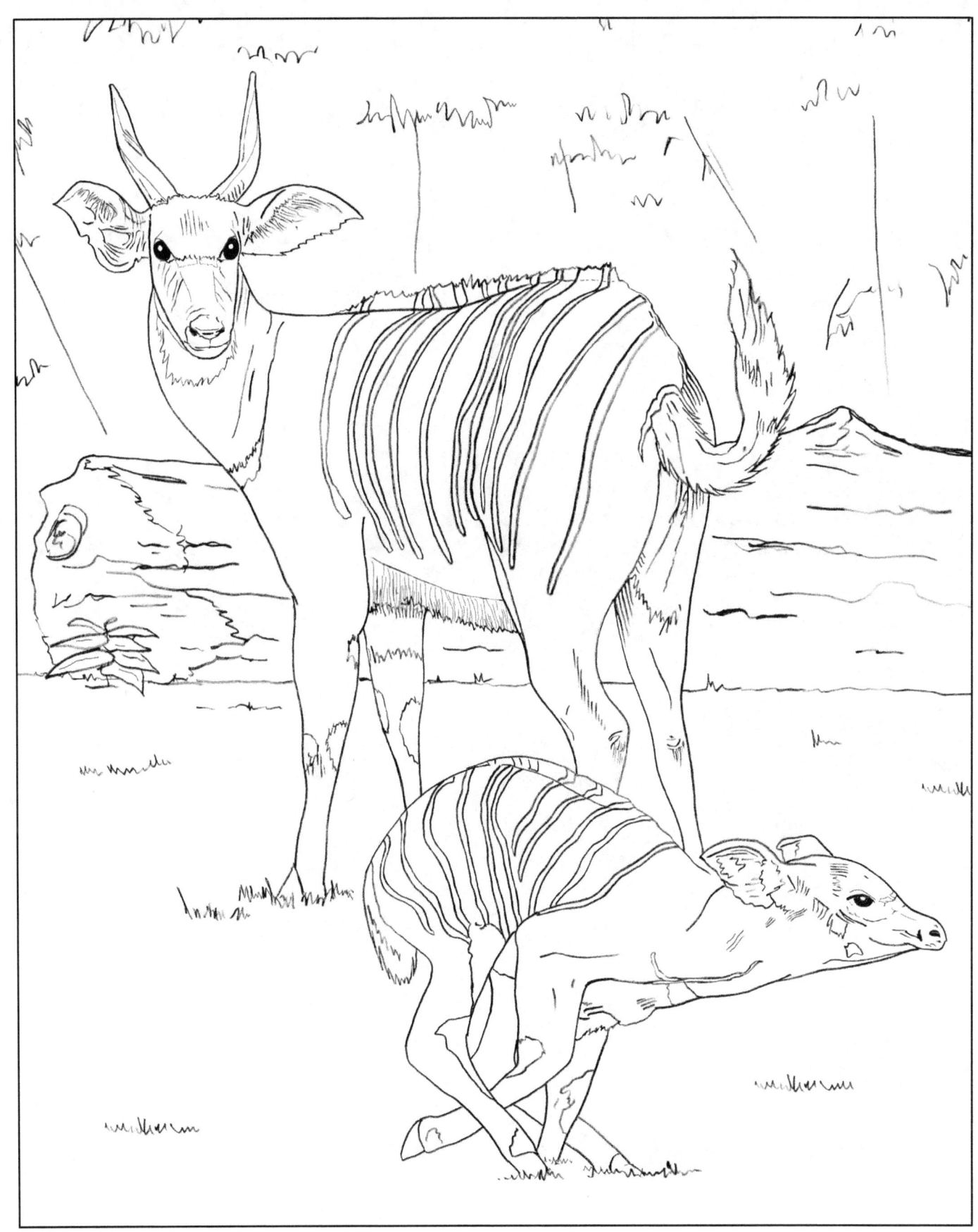

Lowland Nyala
Spiral-horned antelope native to East Africa

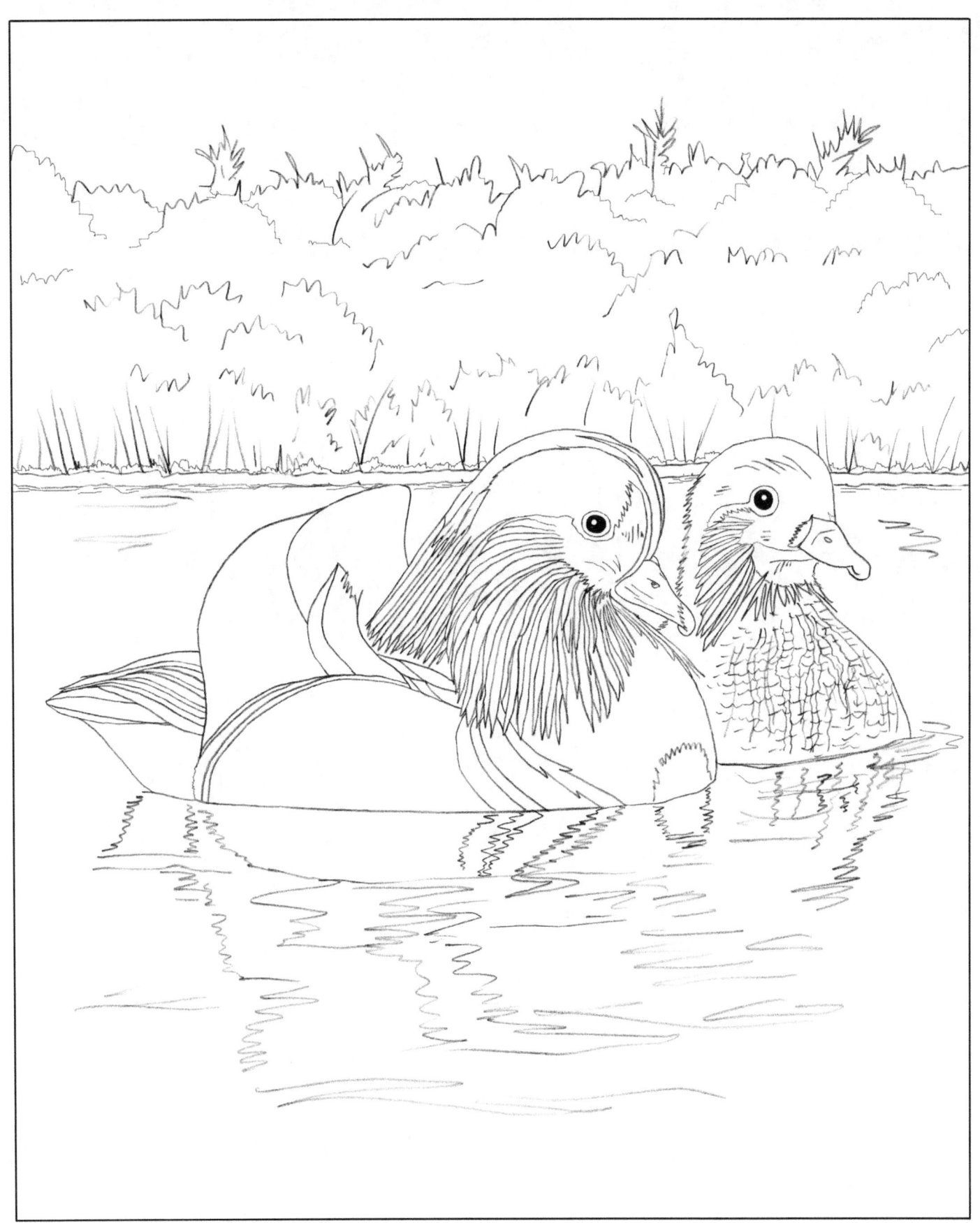

Mandarin Duck
Colorful duck species found in East Asia

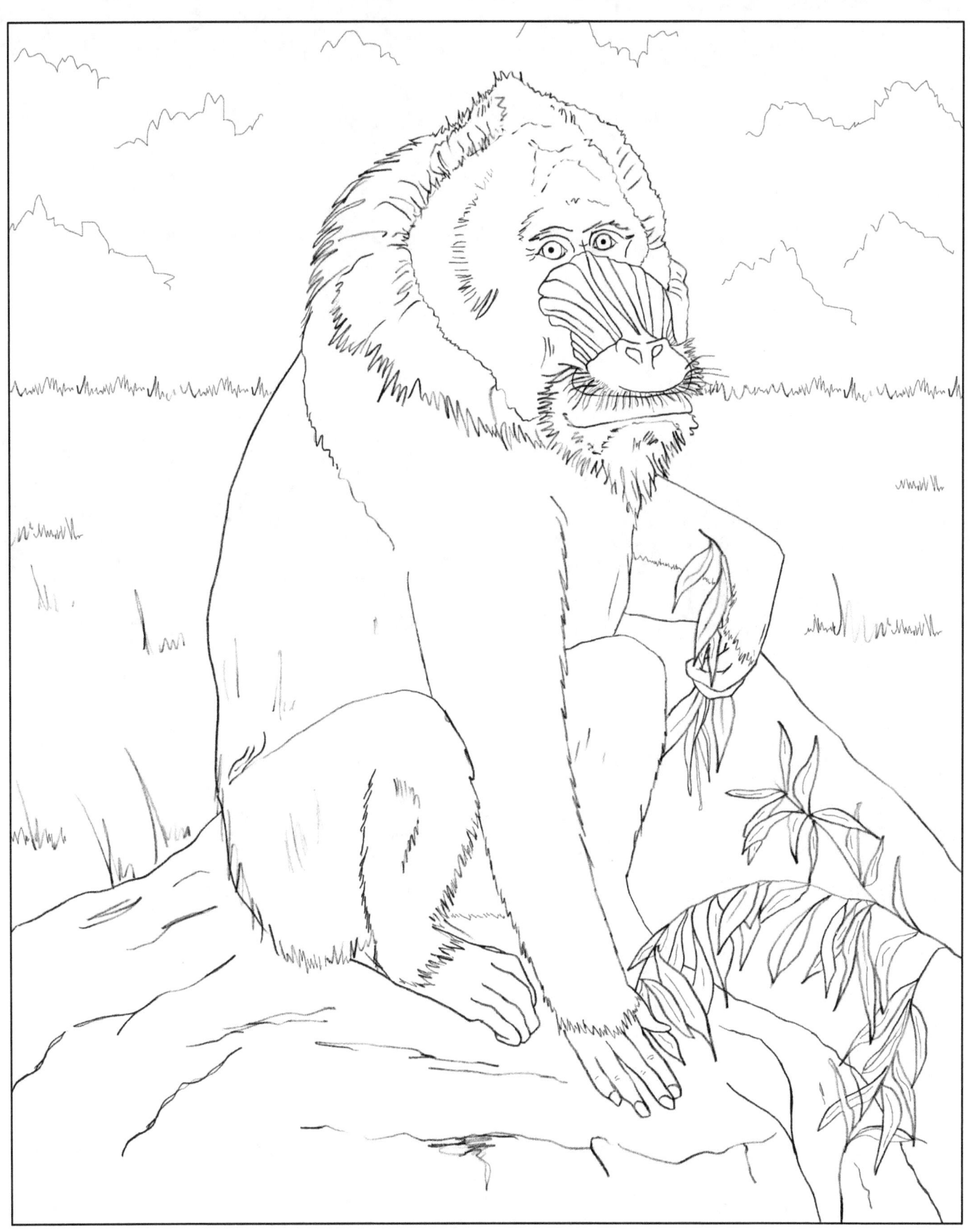

Mandrill Monkey

Mandrills are the world's largest monkeys

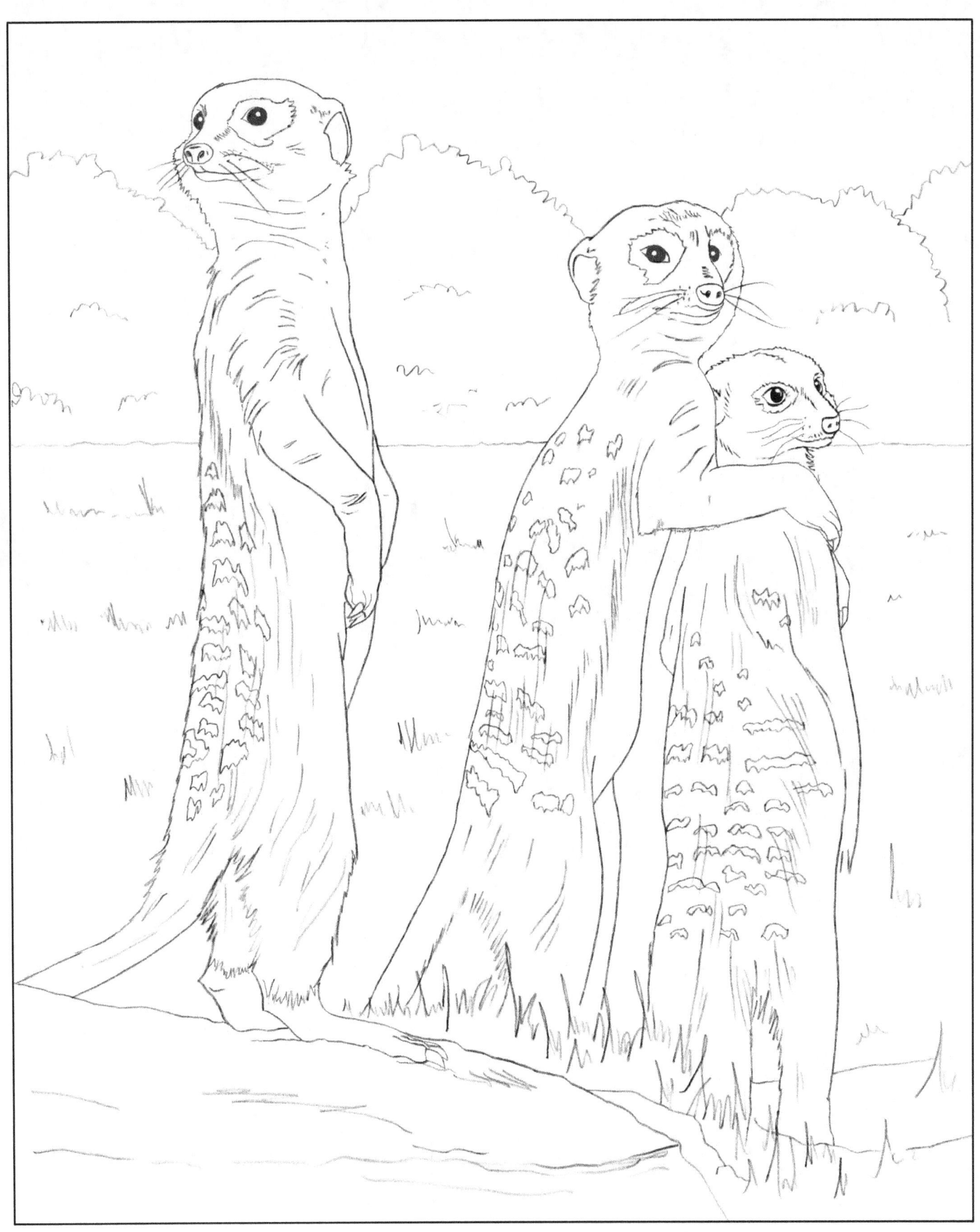

Meerkat
Member of the mongoose family from Africa

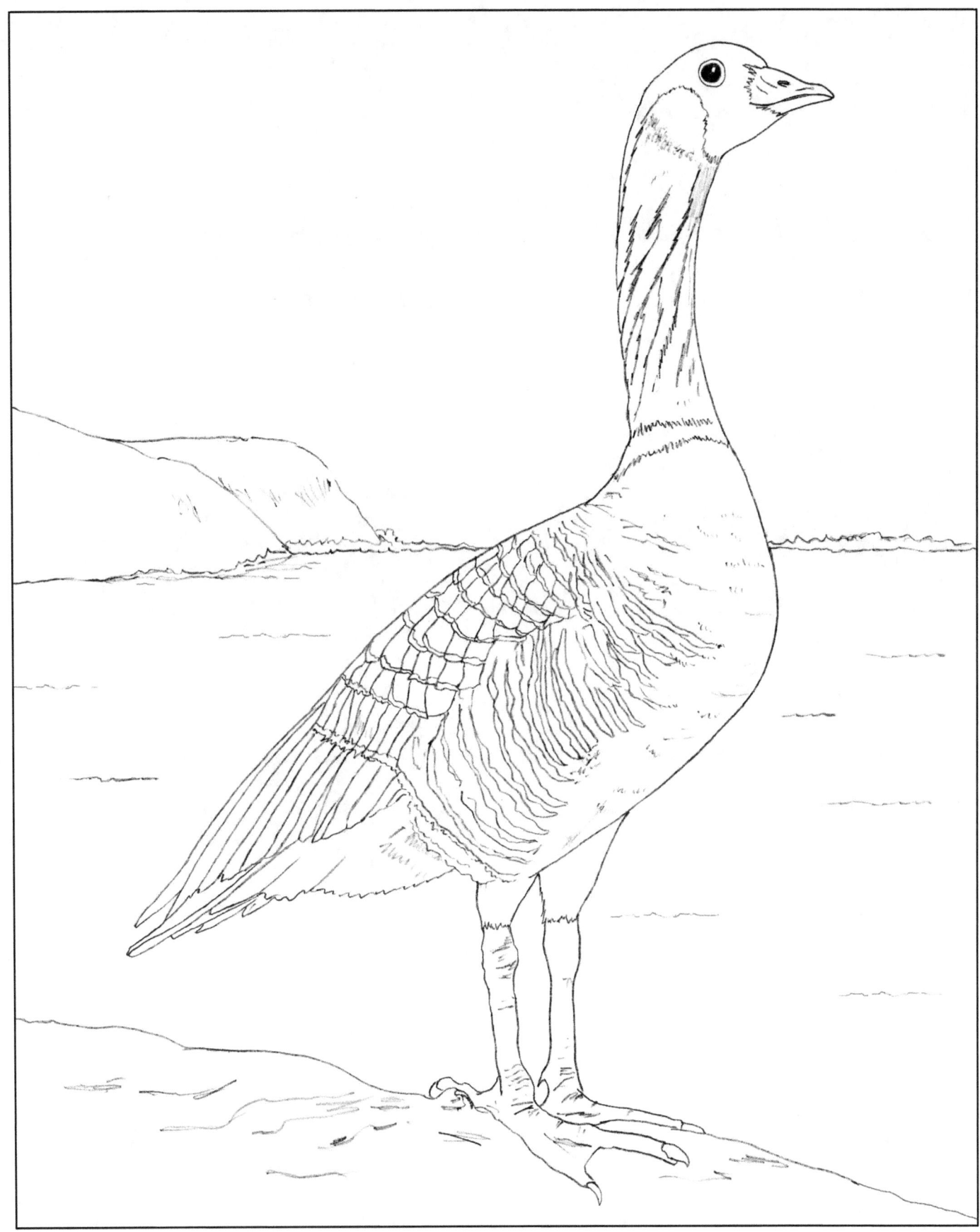

Nene Goose
State Bird of Hawaii

66

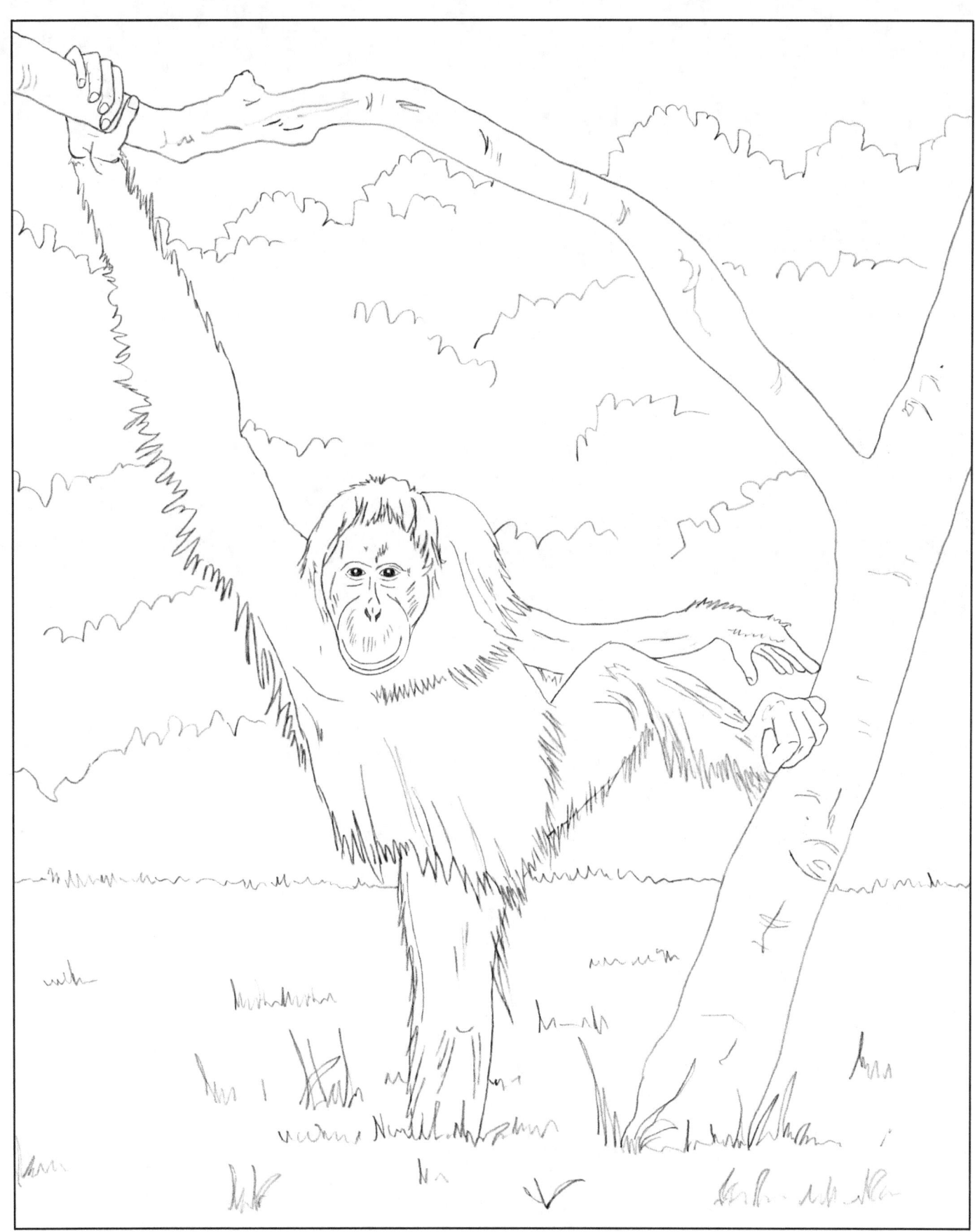

Orangutan
From the rainforests of Borneo

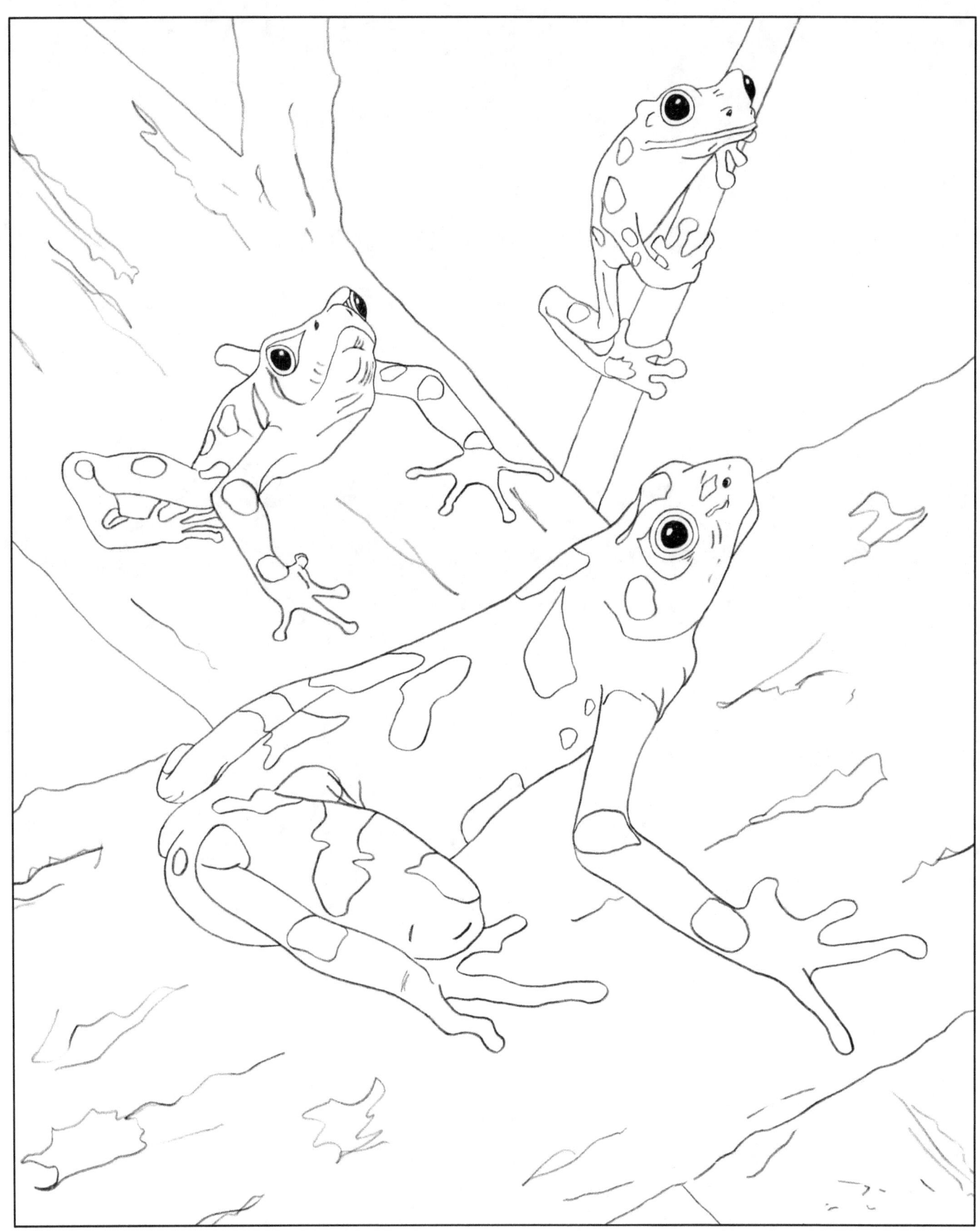

Panamanian Golden Frog
May have been extinct in the wild since 2007

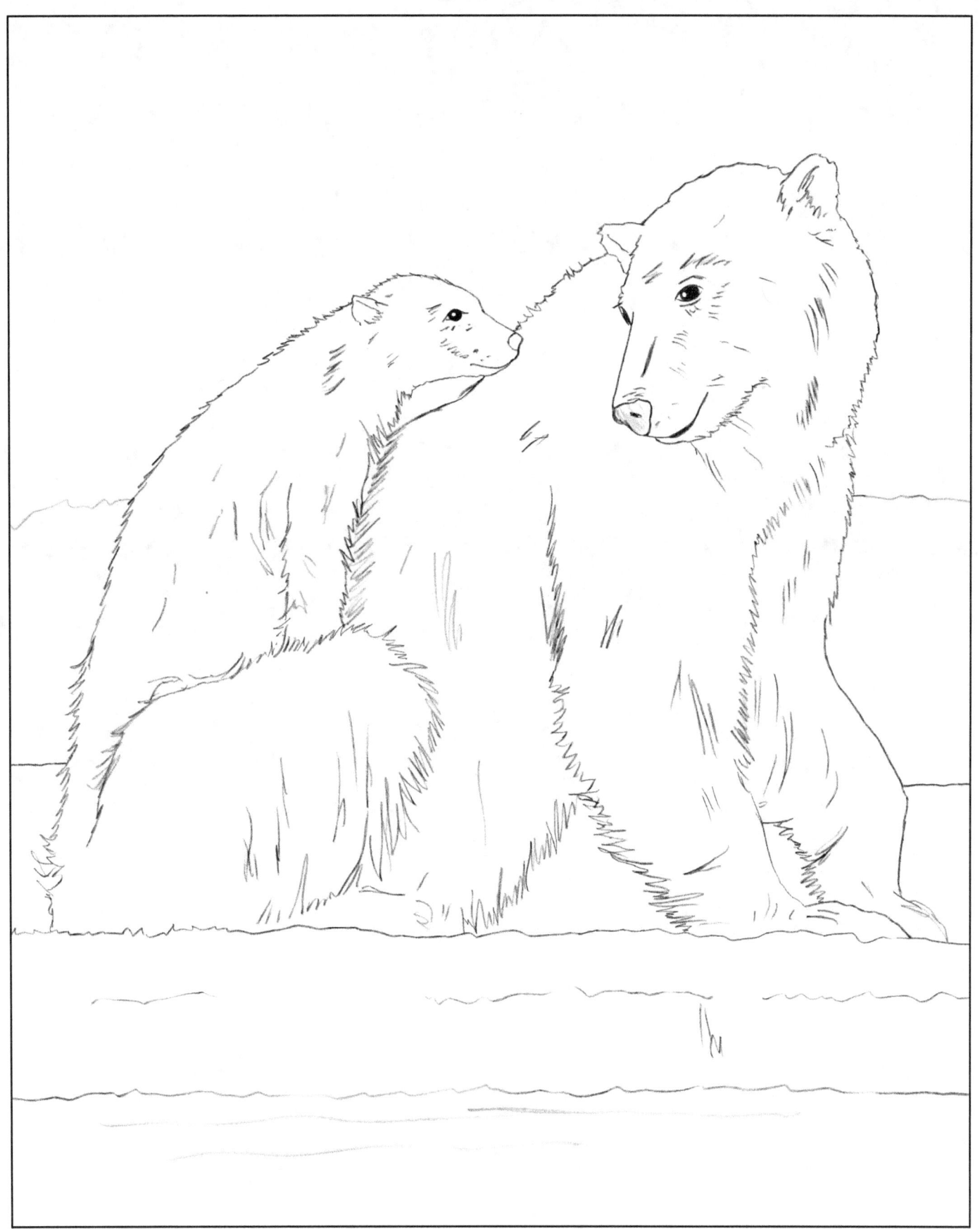

Polar Bear
Polar Bear is a marine mammal from the Arctic Circle

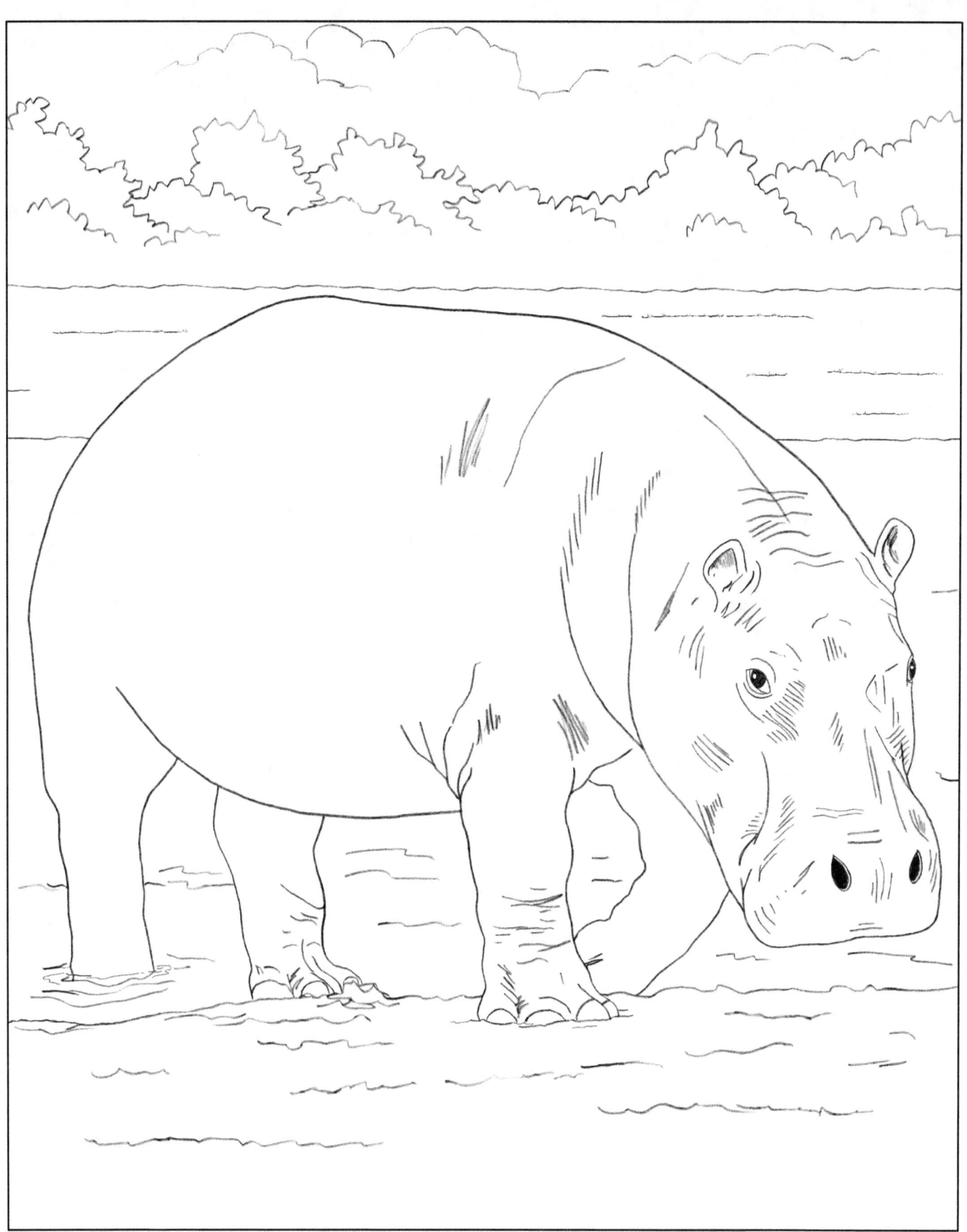

Hippopotamus
Pygmy Hippopotamus from western Africa

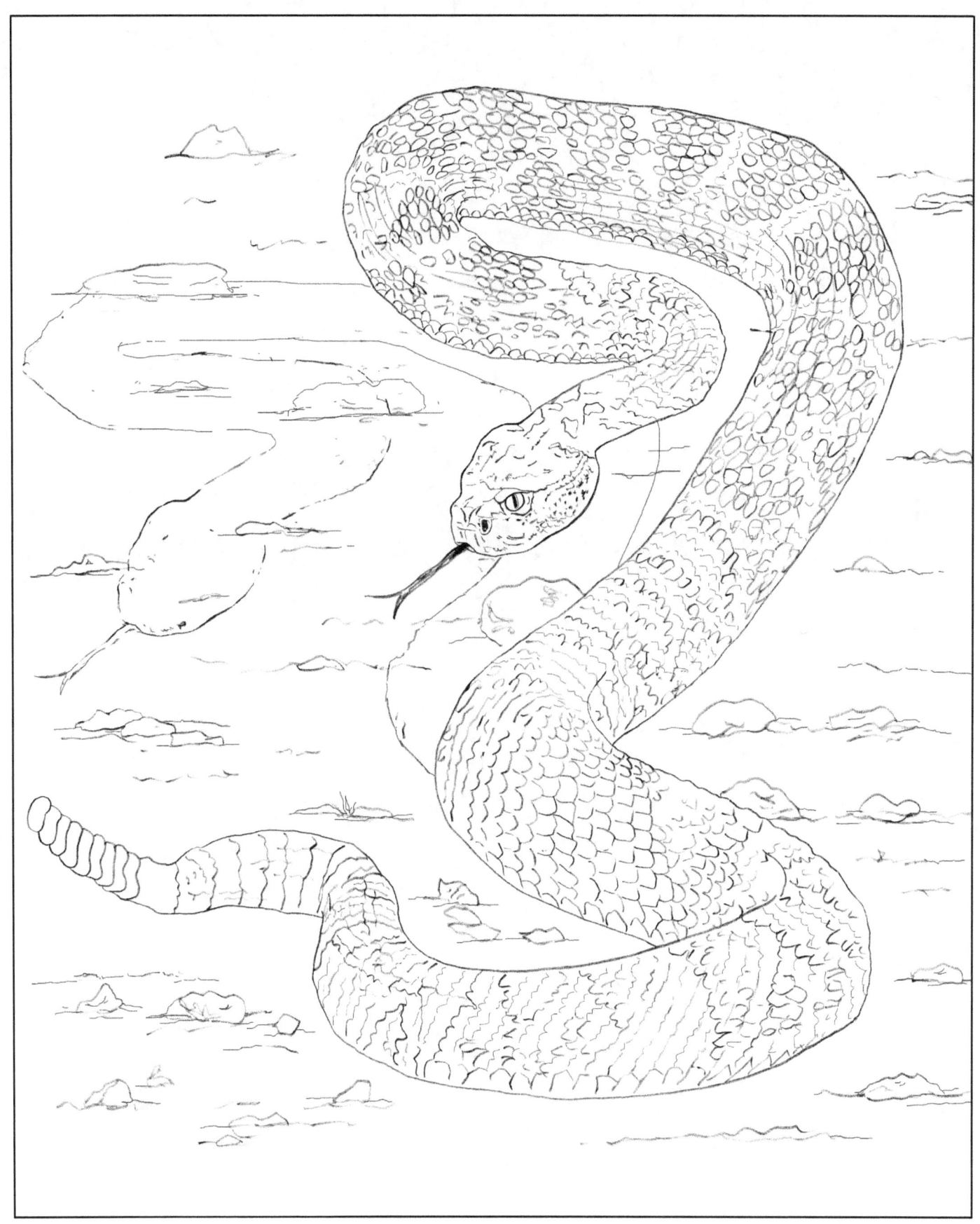

Rattlesnake

Diamondback is most dangerous venomous snake in North America

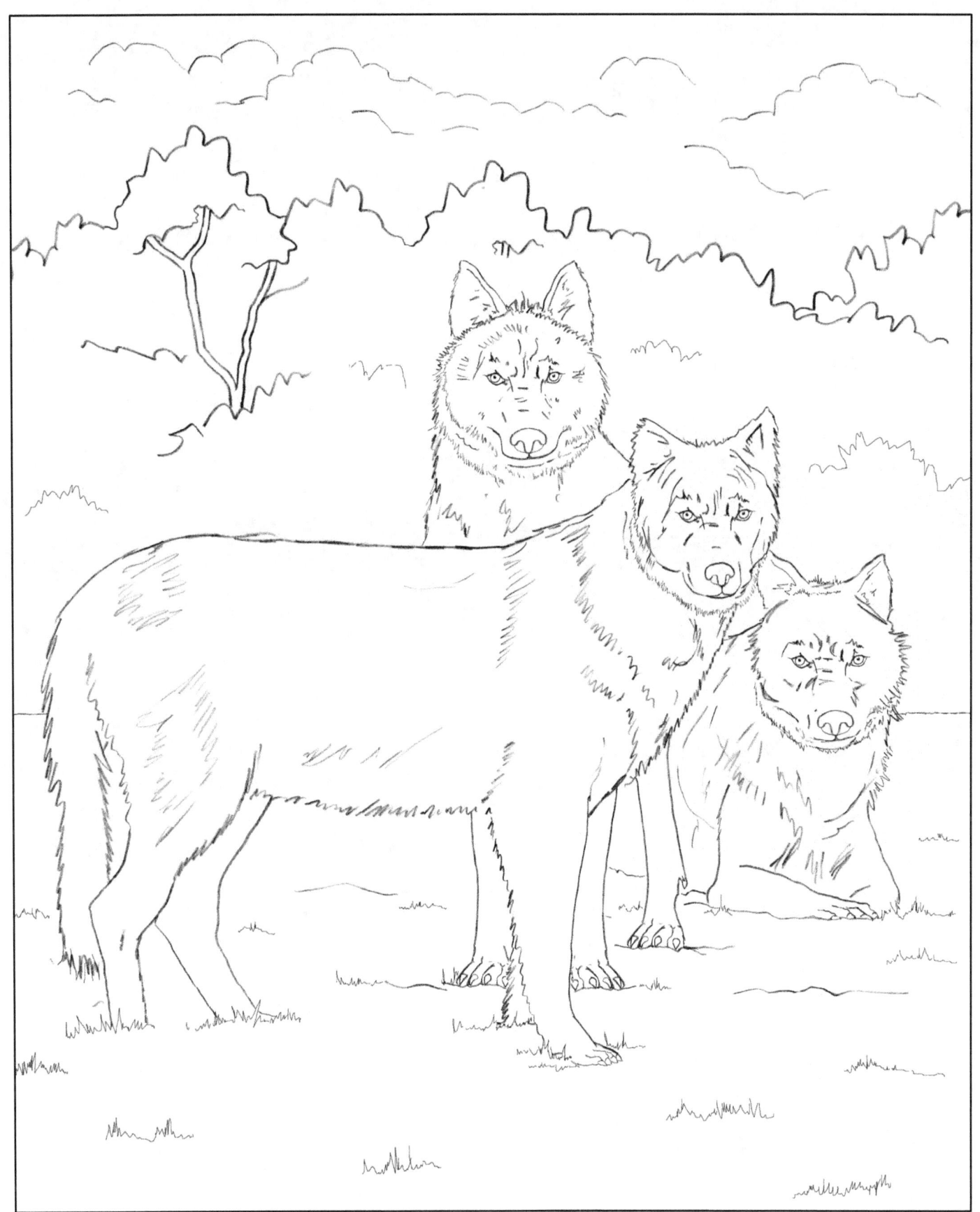

Red Wolf

Nearly driven to extinction by the mid-1900s

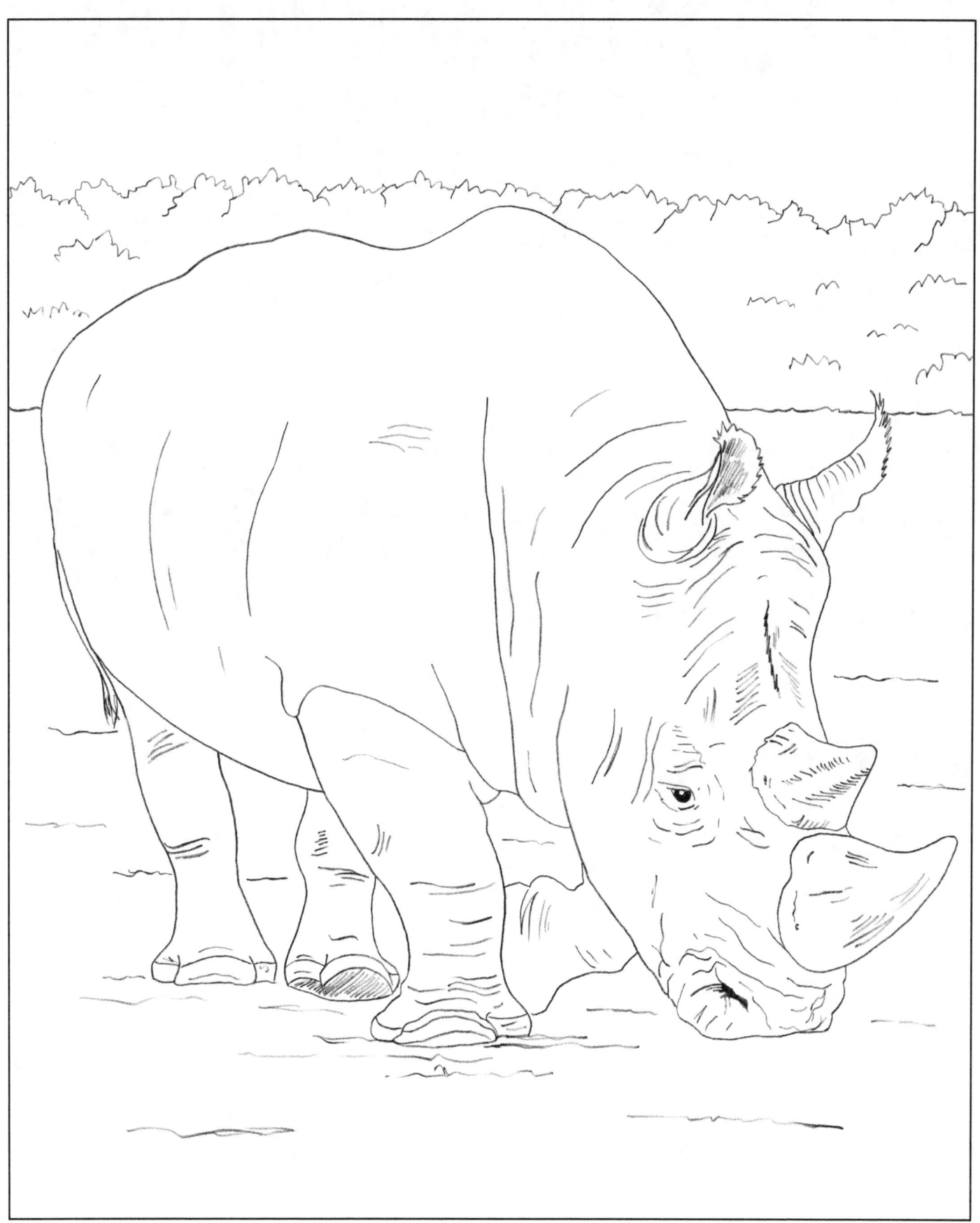

Rhinoceros
The name is derived from two Ancient Greek words for "nose horn"

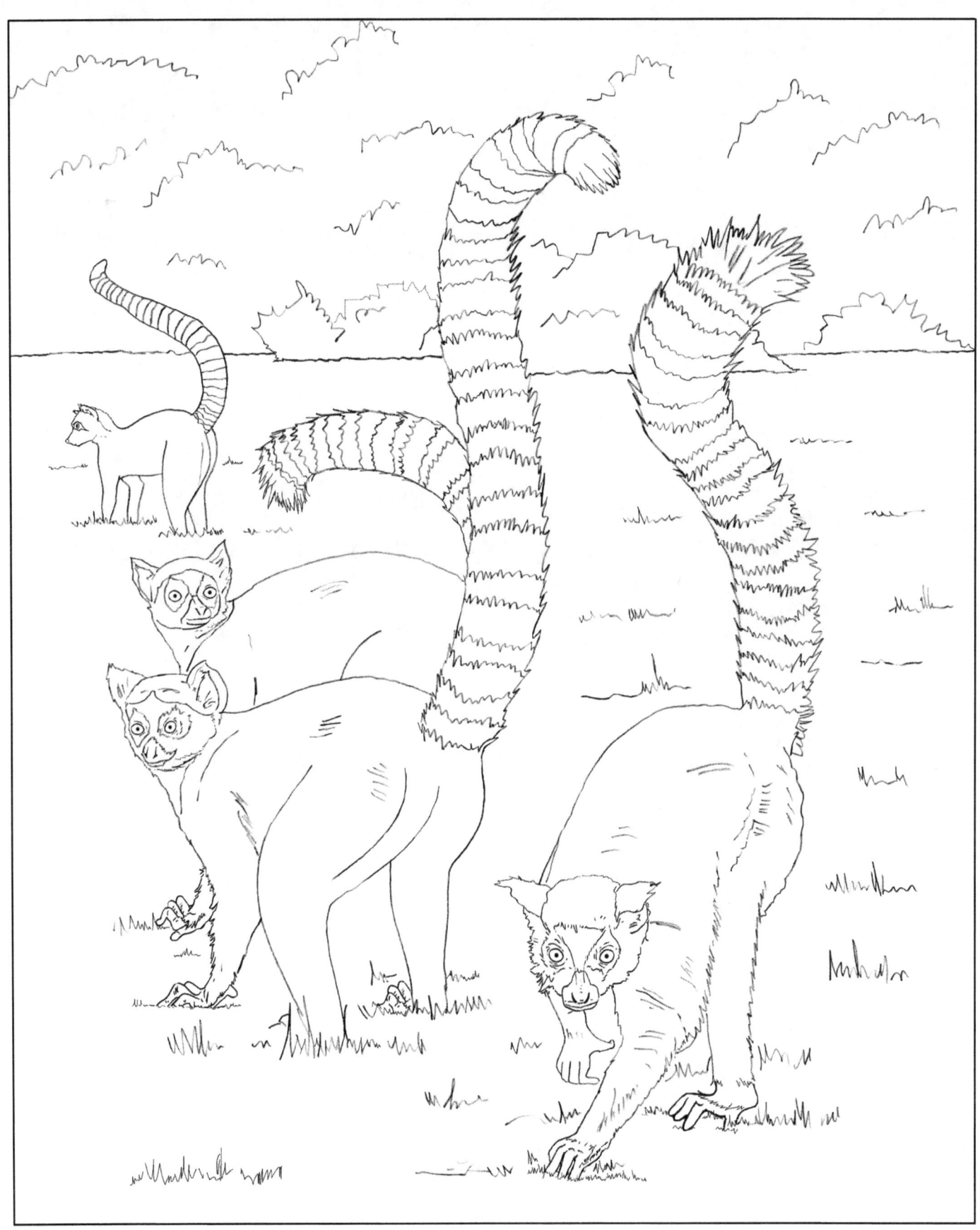

Ring-tailed Lemur
Primate recognized by its long, black and white ringed tail

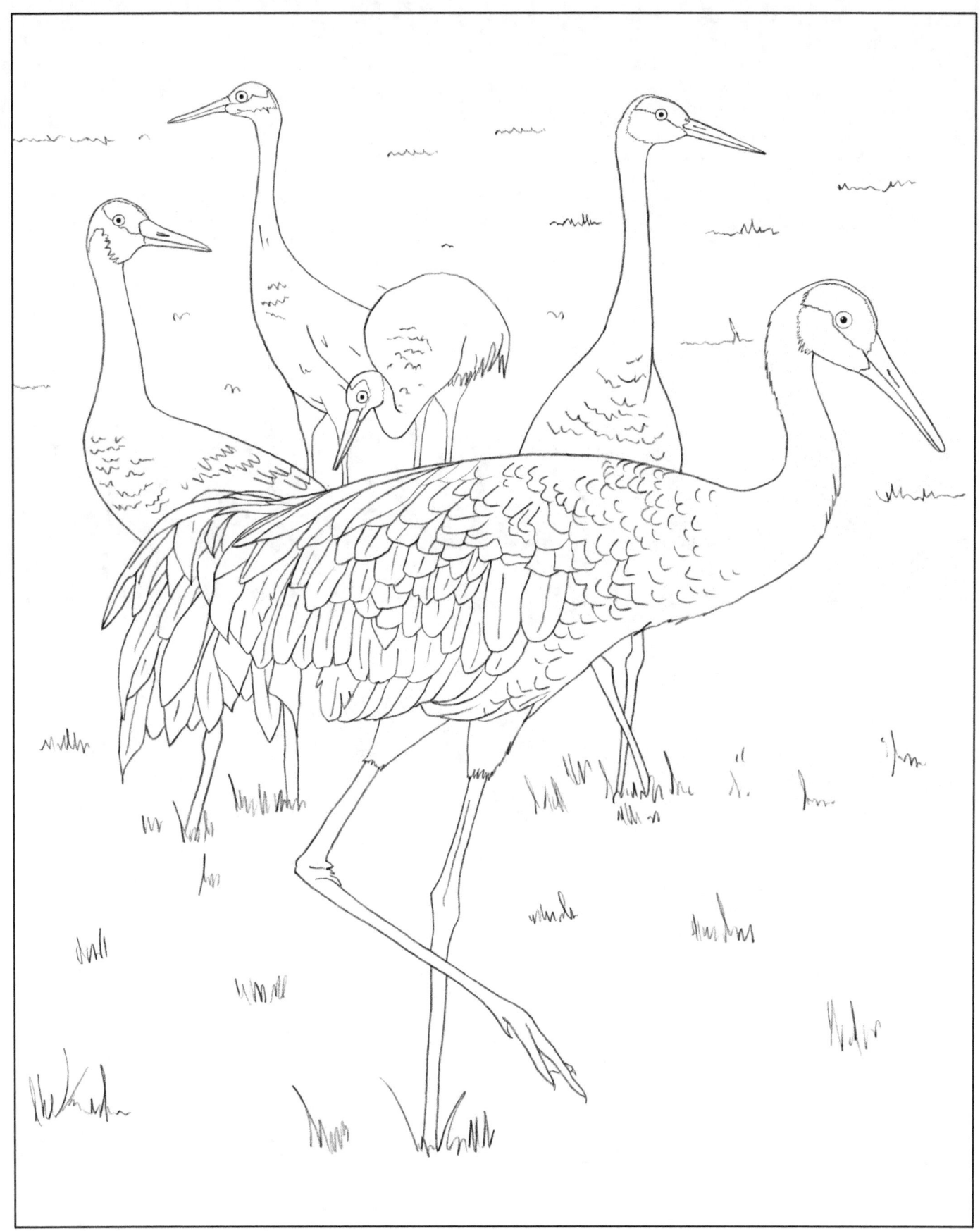

Sandhill Crane
Migrate south for the winter and form enormous flocks

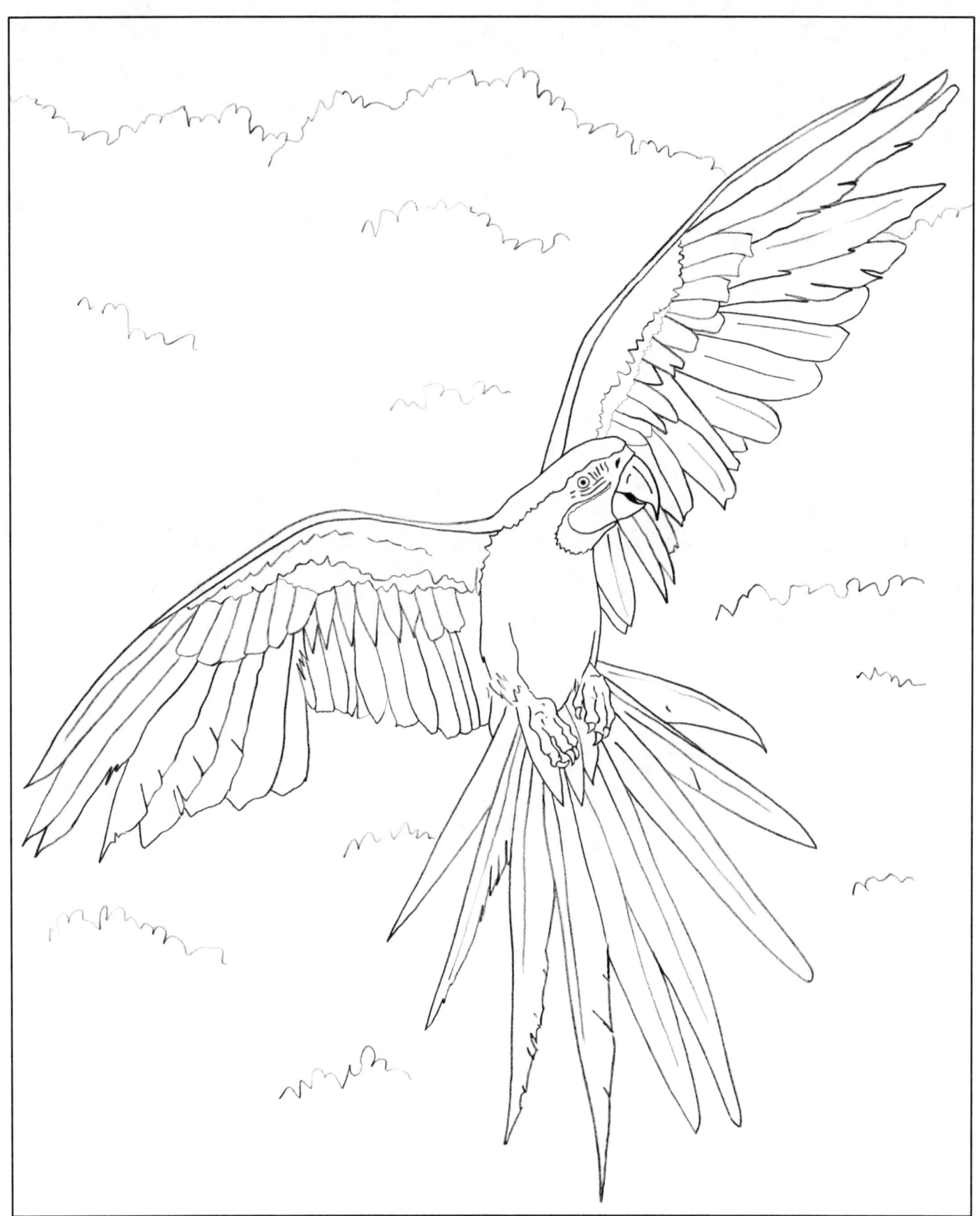

Macaw
From the forests of tropical South America

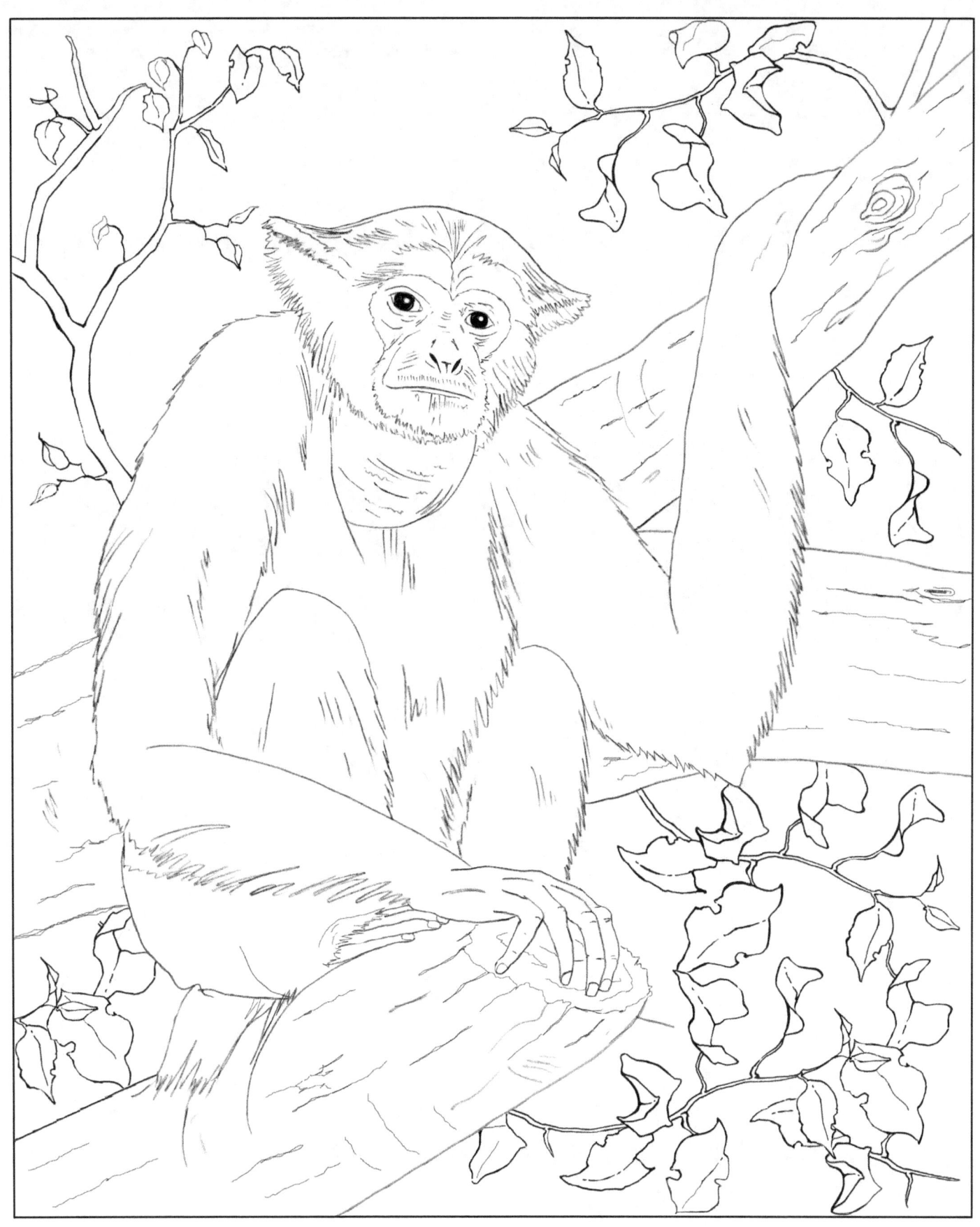

Siamang

Siamang is an arboreal black-furred gibbon

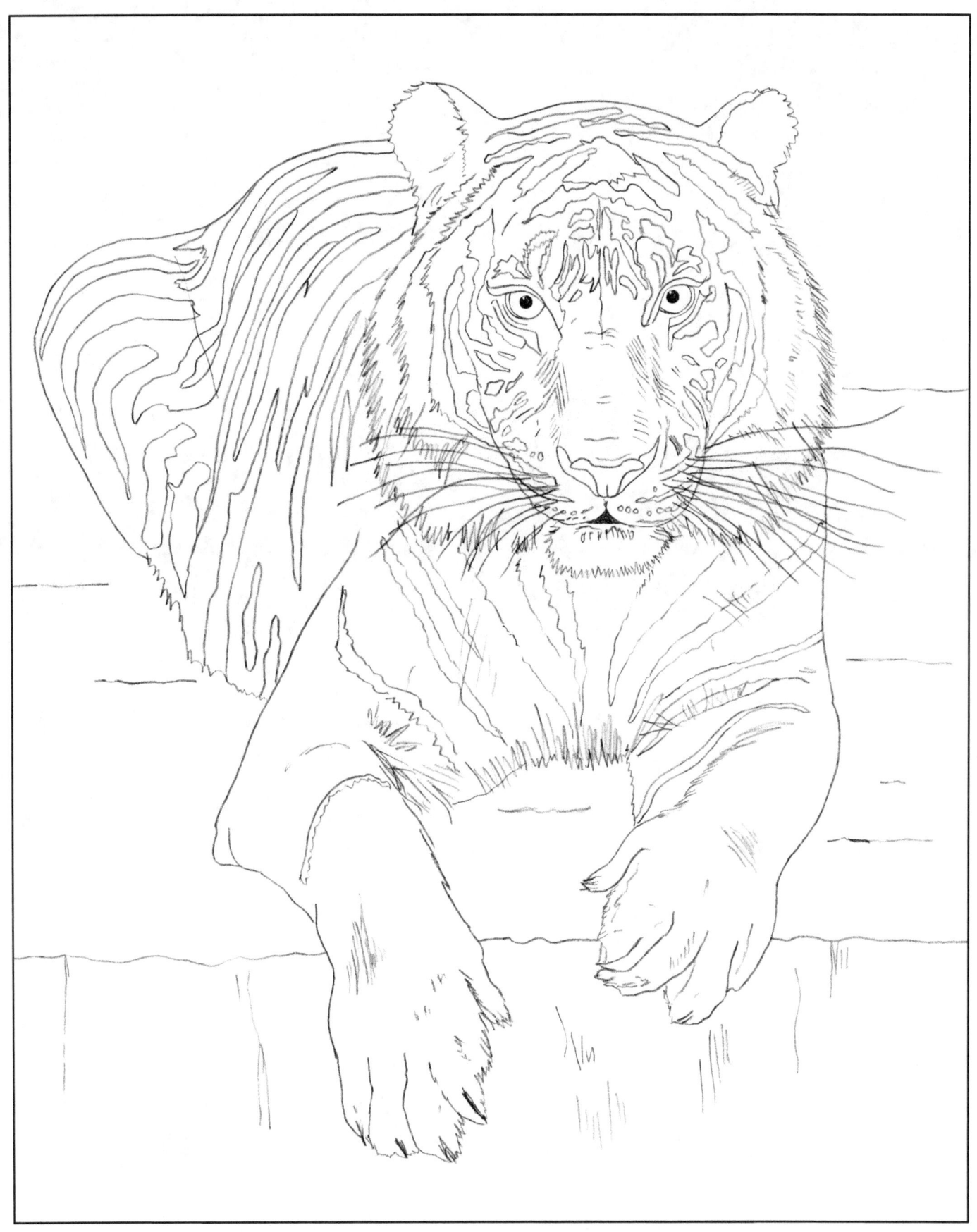

Sumatran Tiger
A rare tiger from the Indonesian island of Sumatra

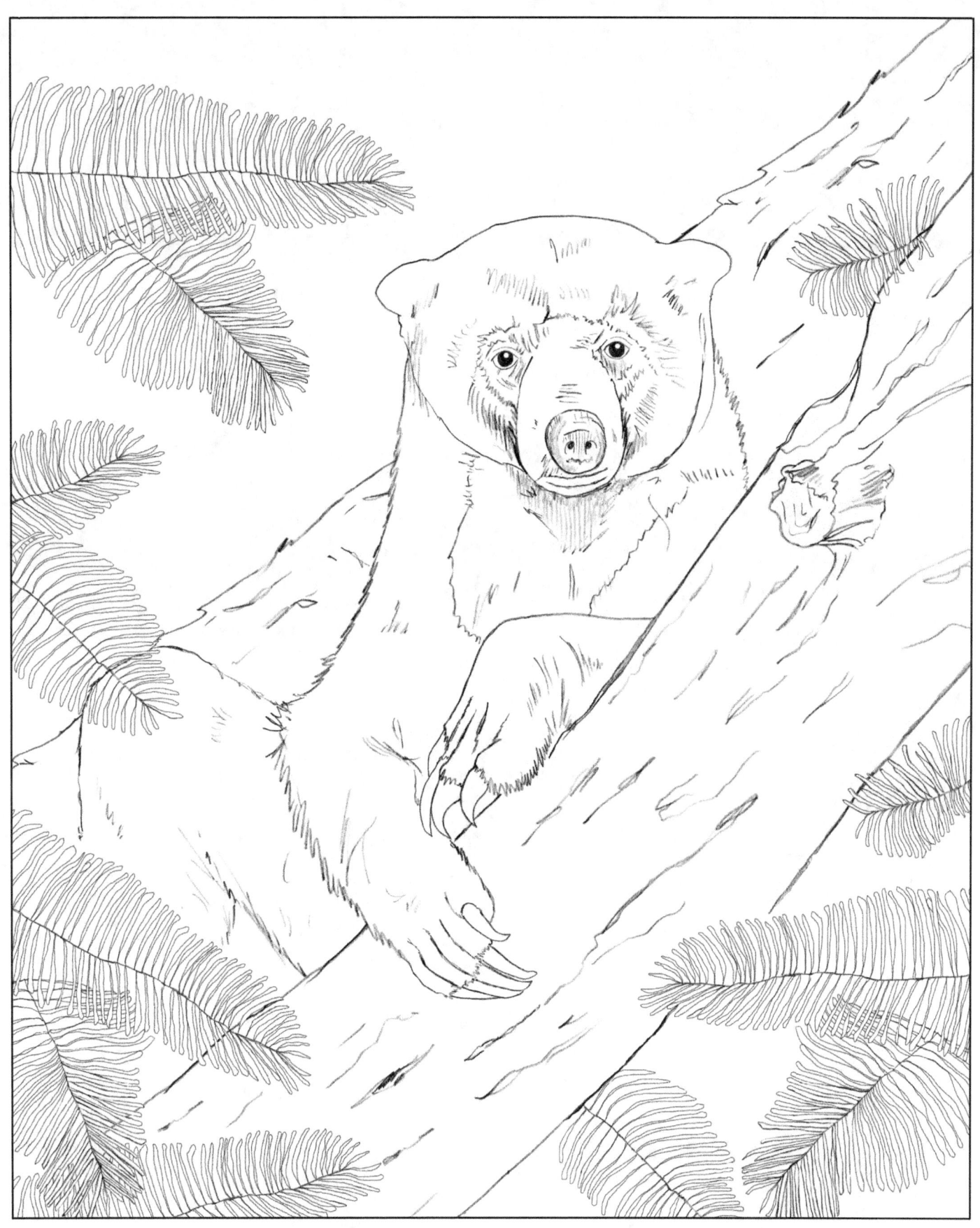

Sun Bear
Also known as the Honey Bear

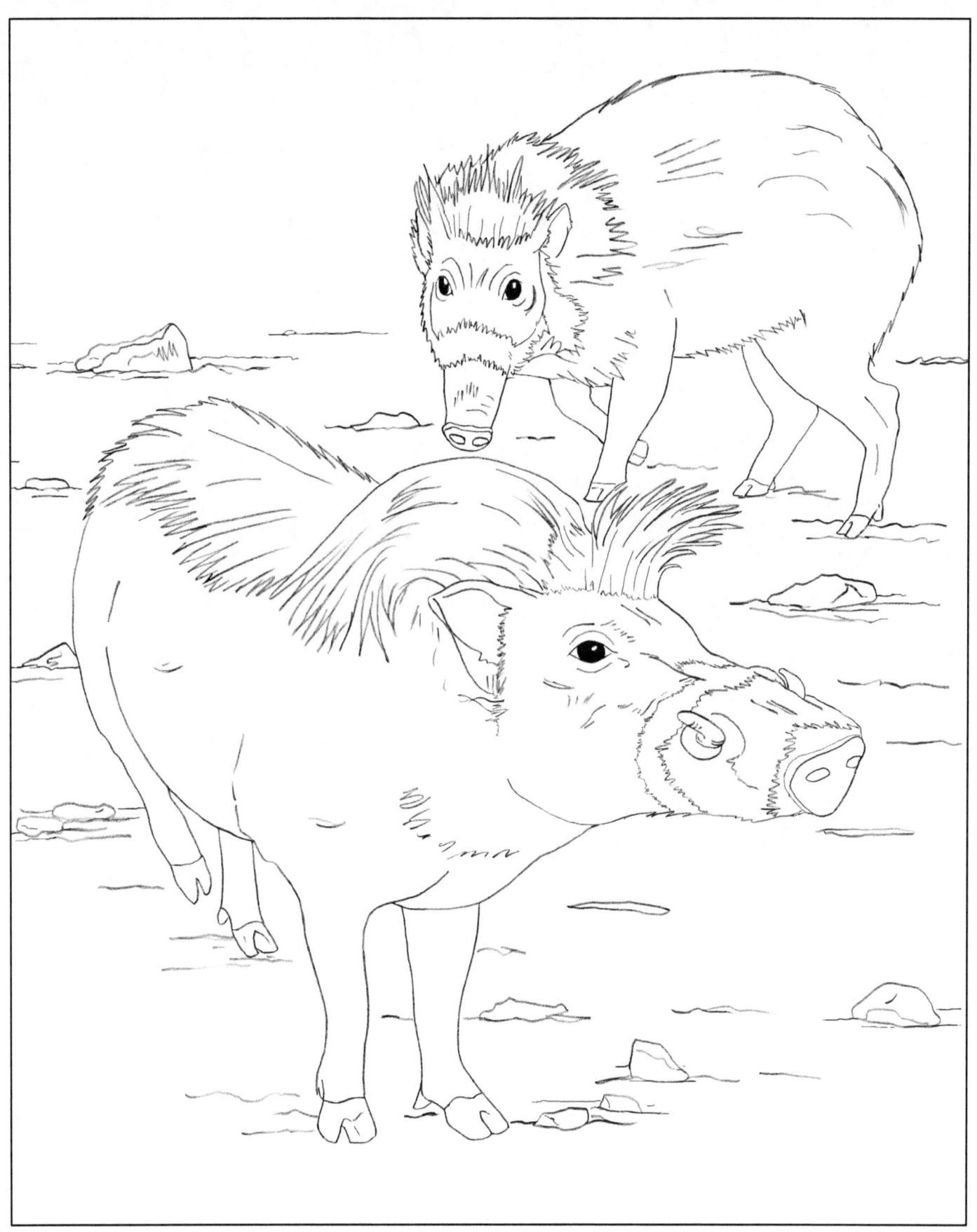

Visayan Warty Hog

From the Visayan Islands in the central Philippines

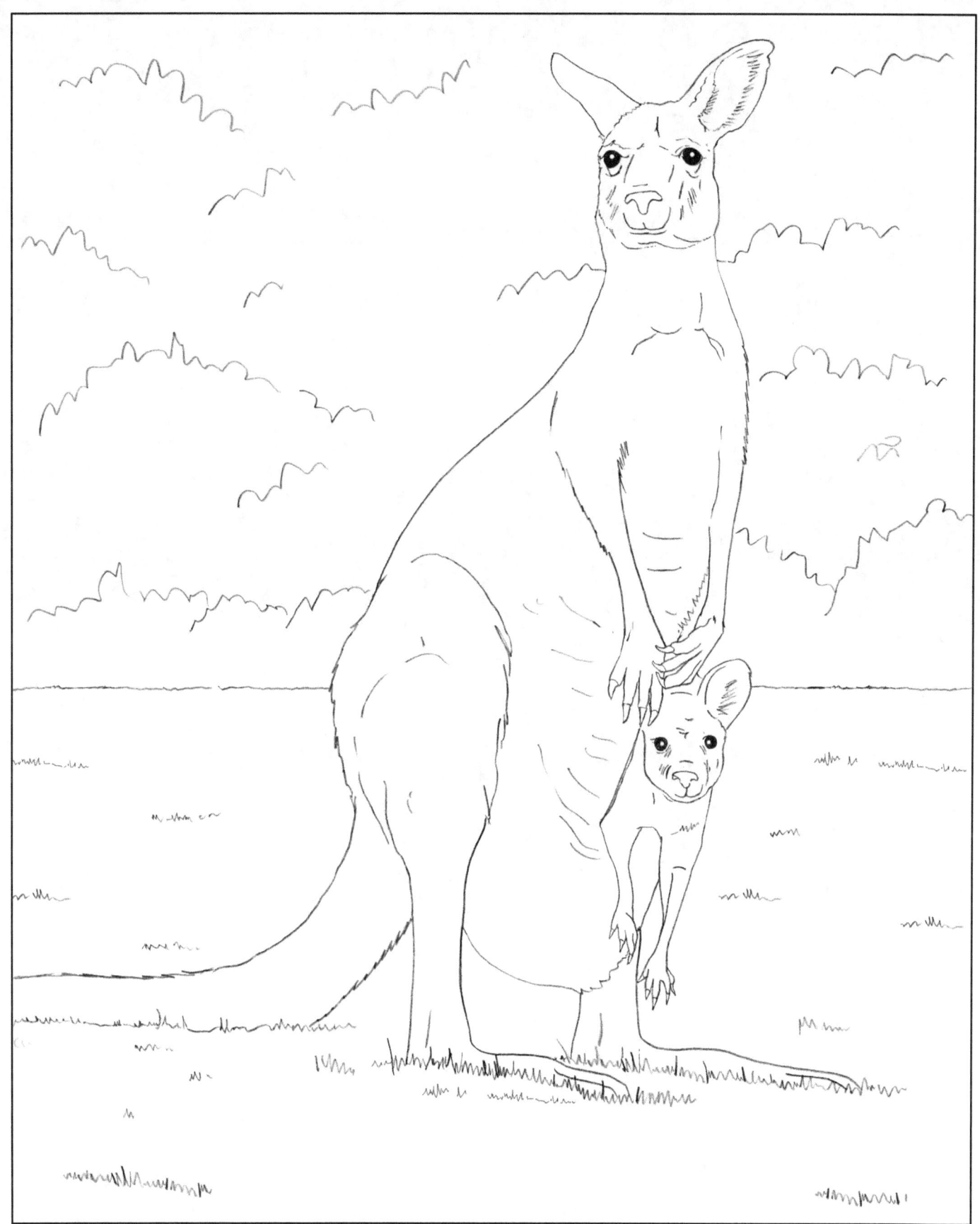

Wallaby
Member of the Kangaroo family from Australia

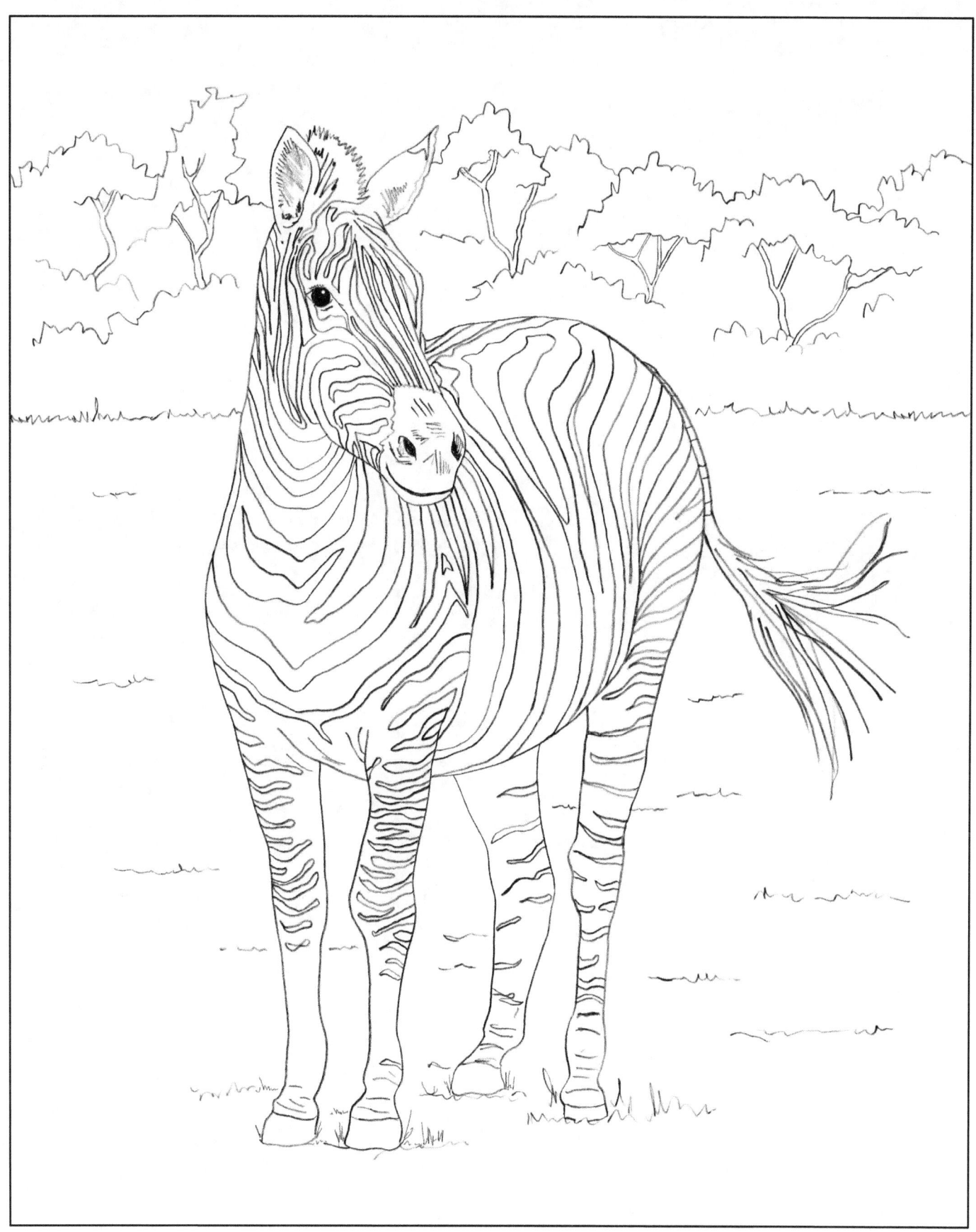

Zebra
Each zebra has its own unique pattern of stripes

Brief Subject Notes

African Elephant is the world's largest living land animal. It is native to the area of Africa south of the Sahara Desert. Elephants have several distinctive features, the most notable of which is a long trunk which is used for many purposes; particularly breathing, lifting water and grasping objects. Their incisors grow into tusks, which can serve as weapons and as tools for moving objects and digging. Their large ears flap to help control their body temperature. Their pillar-like legs can carry their great weight. African elephants have larger ears and concave backs while Asian elephants have smaller ears and level backs. They are an endangered species.

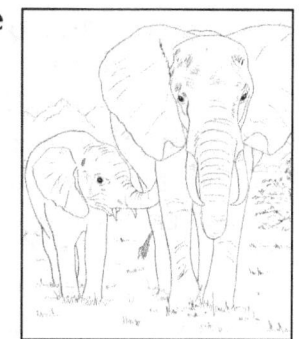

African Penguin is also known as the jackass penguin and black-footed

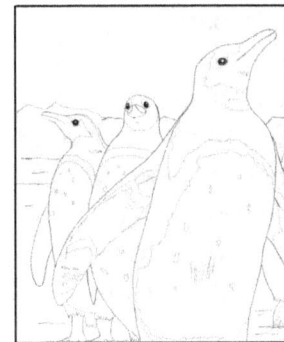

penguin. It is confined to southern African waters and makes a donkey-like bray. Like all penguins, it is flightless, with a streamlined body, and wings stiffened and flattened into flippers for a marine habitat. Adults are 24 to 28 inches tall, very recognizable because of a thick band of black that is in the shape of an upside-down horseshoe. They have black feet and unique black spots that vary in size and shape per penguin. The body upperparts are black and sharply delineated from the white underparts. The African penguin feeds primarily on fish and squid. Once extremely numerous, the African penguin is now classified as endangered.

Amazon Parrots are medium-sized parrots native to South America and the Caribbean vicinity. They feed in small groups throughout the treetops and may even venture to within 6 feet of the ground in their search for food. While life expectancy in the wild is approximately 20 years, some in captivity have been known to live more than 50 years. Most amazon parrots are predominantly green, with accenting colors that can be quite vivid. They feed primarily on seeds, nuts, and fruits, supplemented by leafy matter. Because Amazon parrots have a remarkable ability to mimic human speech and other sounds, they are popular as pets. The Amazon is an endangered species, and the capture of wild parrots is illegal.

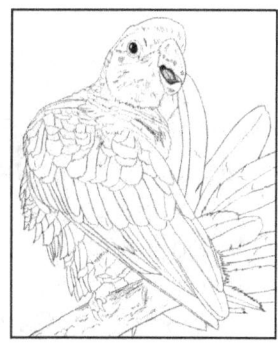

American Alligators are found in the wild in the freshwater wetlands of southeastern United States, from the Great Dismal Swamp in Virginia and North Carolina, south to Everglades National Park in Florida, and west to the southern tip of Texas. Rare White Alligators are considered a symbol of extraordinarily good luck by Eastern mythology. Not all white

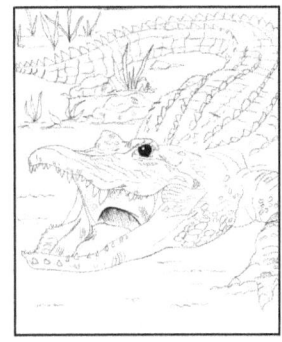

alligators are albino. Albinos have red eyes; another type has blue eyes. The alligator is distinguished from the American crocodile by its broader snout, with overlapping jaws and darker coloration, and is more tolerant of cooler climates than the crocodile, which is only found in tropical climates. Alligators are predators and consume fish, amphibians, reptiles, birds, and mammals. Temperature of the nest determines the sex of the young. The alligator is one of the very few species ever taken off the endangered list.

Bald Eagle is the National bird of the United States of America. A bird of prey found in North America whose range includes most of Canada and Alaska, all of the contiguous United States, and northern Mexico. It is found near large bodies of open water with an abundant food supply and old-growth trees for nesting. The adult is mainly brown with a white head and tail. The beak is large and hooked. Maturity is attained at the age of four to five years. Females are about 25 percent larger than males. In the late 20th century it was on the brink of extinction in the United States. Populations have since recovered and the species was removed from the list of endangered species in 1995 and transferred to the list of threatened species.

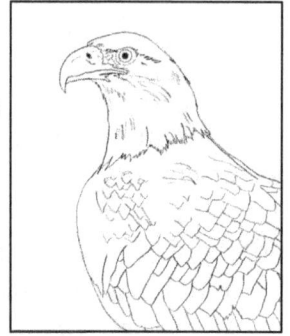

Barn Owl is found in farm communities almost everywhere in the world except polar and desert regions. It can be distinguished from other owls by its unique shape, color, and voice.

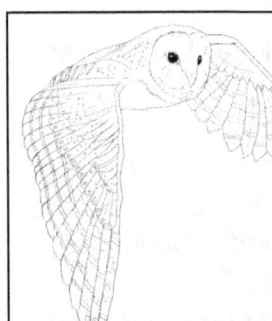

It has long feathered legs with white, buff, yellow, and tawny shadings. The plumage on head and back is a mottled gray or brown, underparts vary from white to brown and are speckled with dark markings. The face is characteristically heart-shaped and is white in most cases. This owl does not hoot but utters an eerie, drawn-out shriek. The Barn Owl hunts in areas rich in rodents; in trees and buildings in farm areas, marshes, temperate forests, and grasslands. They can grow to a length of 18 inches, weigh about 1 pound, and have a wingspan up to 43 inches. A barn owl family can eat up to 25,000 mice in a year. It has been called the "golden owl" due to its delicately freckled dark specks and the blending of colors in daylight.

The **Camel** is an even-toed hoofed mammal bearing distinctive fatty deposits known as "humps" on its back. The three surviving species of camel are the Dromedary, or one-humped camel, the Bactrian, or two-humped camel; and the critically endangered wild Bactrian camel in remote areas of northwest China and Mongolia. Both the Dromedary and the Bactrian camels have been domesticated; they provide milk, meat, hair for textiles or goods such as felted pouches, and are working animals with tasks ranging from human transport to bearing loads. Ninety-four percent of the world's camels are Dromedaries. **Camels** have a 3-chambered stomach. They live in arid grassland areas and deserts and can drink 30 gallons of water in about 10 minutes. Camels have huge feet with soft pads for walking on sand. They can carry up to 600 pounds and cover 30 miles in a day.

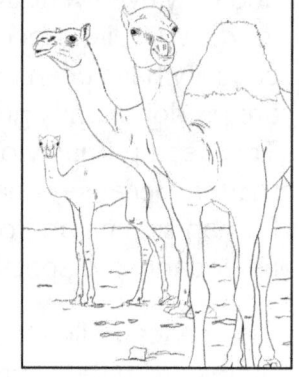

The **Cheetah** is found in eastern and southern Africa and a few parts of Iran. It has a slender body, deep chest, spotted coat, a small rounded head, black tear-like streaks on the face, long thin legs and a long spotted tail. Their lightly built, slender form is in sharp contrast with the robust build of the big cats, making the cheetah more similar to the cougar. The cheetah reaches 28 to 35 inches high at the shoulder. Though taller than the leopard, it is notably smaller than the lion. Basically yellowish tan or rufous to grayish white, the coat is uniformly covered with nearly 2,000 solid black spots. Cheetahs are active mainly during the day, with hunting their major activity; they mainly prey upon antelopes and gazelles. It is the fastest land animal, reaching a speed of 70 mph during a hunting chase.

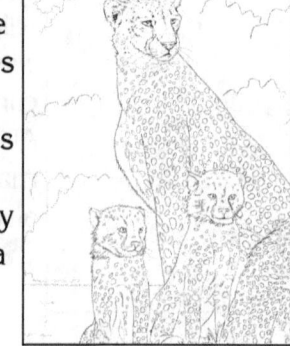

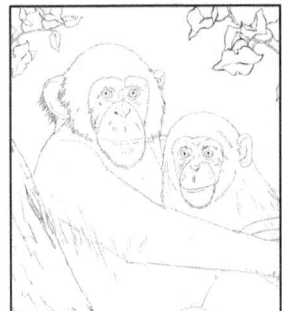

Chimpanzees are part of the Great Ape family from the Congo. They are our closest living relatives, sharing more than 98 percent of our genetic blueprint. Humans and chimps are also thought to share a common ancestor millions of years ago. Chimpanzees live in social communities of several dozen animals. Although they normally walk on all fours (knuckle-walking), chimpanzees can stand and walk upright. By swinging from branch to branch they can also move quite efficiently in the trees, where they do most of their eating. Chimpanzees usually sleep in the trees as well, employing nests of leaves. A chimpanzee's arms are longer than its legs. The male chimp stands up to 3.9 feet high and weighs as much as 200 pounds. The chimpanzee is tailless; its coat is dark; its face, fingers, palms of the hands, and soles of the feet are hairless.

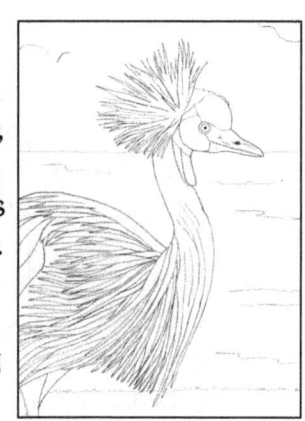

The **East African Crowned Crane** is found in the dry savannah in Africa south of the Sahara. The grey crowned crane is the national bird of Uganda and featured in the country's flag and coat of arms. It is listed as endangered. They live in groups of up to 150 birds and are monogamous, having the same partner for life. Parents teach their offspring dances and calls. The behaviors are not instinctual. This crane has a chin wattle that is used to create calls to summon its mate. It can be heard from miles away. Yellow crowns are used as camouflage in the tall, yellow grasses of Africa. Their windpipe is five feet long, half of which is coiled in the breastbone. This allows them to produce loud, trombone-like calls that carry over long distances. The crowned crane is the only crane that perches in trees.

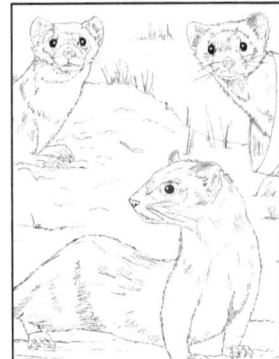

The endangered **Black-footed Ferret** is a member of the weasel family. It is the only ferret native to North America; the domestic ferret is of European origin. Black-footed ferrets once numbered in the tens of thousands across the great plains from southern Canada to Mexico but were considered extinct by the 1960s. Although still endangered, they are making a comeback. Approximately 20 zoos across the country now exhibit the black-footed ferret and are part of the program to reproduce and release them into the wild. The black-footed ferret has a tan body with black legs and feet, a black tip on the tail and a black mask. The ferret has short legs with large front paws and claws developed for digging. Its large skull and strong jaw and teeth are adapted for eating meat. Black-footed ferrets spend about 90 percent of their time underground, where they eat, sleep and raise their young in prairie dog burrows. They are nocturnal and leave their burrows at night to hunt prairie dogs.

The **Greater Flamingo** is found in Africa, on the Indian subcontinent, in the Middle East and southern Europe. This is the largest species of flamingo, averaging 4 - 5 feet tall. Male flamingos have been recorded at over 6 feet tall. It is closely related to the American flamingo and Chilean flamingo. All flamingos lay a single chalky-white egg on a mud mound. Most of the plumage is pinkish-white, but the wing coverts are red and the primary and secondary flight feathers are black. The bill is pink with a restricted black tip, and the legs are entirely pink. The call is a goose-like honking. The bird resides in mudflats and shallow coastal lagoons with salt water. Using its feet, the bird stirs up the mud, then sucks water through its bill and filters out small shrimp, seeds, blue-green algae, microscopic organisms and mollusks.

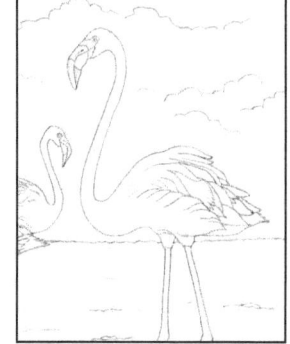

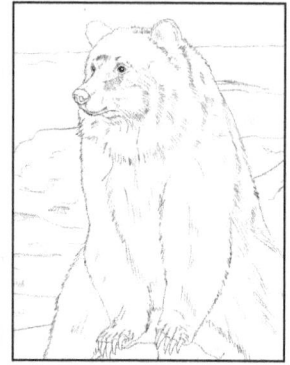

Florida Black Bear is a subspecies of the American black bear that has historically ranged throughout most of Florida and southern portions of Alabama, Georgia, and Mississippi. They are typically large-bodied with shiny black fur, a light brown nose, and a short stubby tail. It is currently Florida's largest terrestrial mammal with an average male weight of 300 pounds. Average adults have a length of between 4 feet and 6 feet. Florida black bears are mainly solitary, except when in groups or pairings during mating season. Most are not territorial, and typically do not defend their range from other bears. Black bears have good eyesight, acute hearing and an excellent sense of smell. Florida black bears live mainly in forested habitats and are common in sand-pine scrub, oak scrub, upland hardwood forests and forested wetlands.

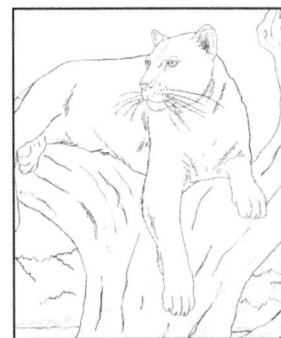

Florida Panther was chosen in 1982 as the Florida state animal. It is an endangered subspecies of cougar that lives in forests and swamps of southern Florida. It is often referred to as cougar, mountain lion, puma, and catamount, but the Florida panther is distinctively different from cougar subspecies found in other regions of the United States. In the 1970s, there were an estimated 20 Florida panthers in the wild, and their numbers have increased to an estimated 160 as of 2016. Florida panthers are spotted at birth and typically have blue eyes. As the panther grows the spots fade and the coat becomes completely tan while the eyes typically take on a yellow hue. The panther's underbelly is a creamy white, and it has black tips on the tail and ears. Florida panthers lack the ability to roar, and instead growls, hisses, and purrs.

Masai Giraffe is found in central and southern Kenya and in Tanzania. The giraffe is a genus of African even-toed hoofed mammals, the tallest living terrestrial animals. They have brown leaf-shaped blotches on their tan coat. Offspring are six feet tall at birth. The mother gives birth while standing and the young fall six feet to the ground upon delivery. Giraffes usually stay in small herds of 15 to 20 called a family group. They run up to 30 mph. Sleeping is usually done standing up, but resting is done in a sitting position. Giraffes get spooked easily, but their legs are powerful enough to break concrete when used in defense. Head horns are present at birth but only used in male-to-male combat. Their long neck has only seven vertebrae (the same as humans).

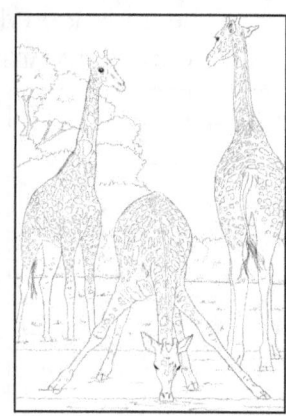

Gorillas are ground-dwelling, predominantly herbivorous apes that inhabit the forests of central Africa. The genus is divided into two species: the eastern gorillas and the western gorillas (both critically endangered). They are the world's largest living primates. The DNA of gorillas is highly similar to that of humans, from 95 to 99%; the next closest living relatives to humans after the chimpanzees. Gorillas live in family groups of anywhere from 2 to 20 individuals. The silverback is the dominant, mature male. He makes decisions concerning where and when to eat and sleep and protects the family from danger. He has the reproductive privileges with the adult females. Gorillas normally walk on all fours with the front knuckles of their hands curled under to support their weight. Their thumbs and big toes are opposable. Gorillas can be identified individually by their unique noseprints (the shape of the nostrils and the pattern of crinkles on the bridges of their noses).

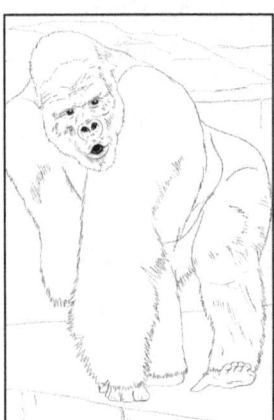

The **Green-naped Rainbow Lorikeet** is one of the most colorful members of the parrot family. It occurs naturally in Australia, as well as on islands north and east of Australia. They can also be found in Indonesia, Papua New Guinea, Solomon Islands, New Zealand, and New Caledonia, where they inhabit rainforests, open forests, woodlands, and mangroves. These social parrots are usually seen in flocks. They are small to medium-sized parrots characterized by their brush-tipped tongues for feeding on nectar of various blossoms and soft fruits, preferably berries. They have very brightly colored plumage. Juveniles have a black beak, which gradually brightens to orange in the adults.

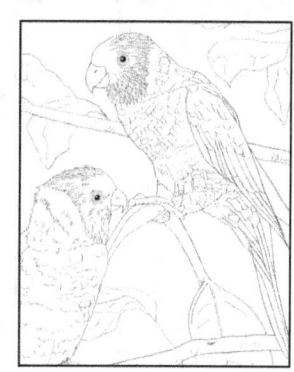

The **Impala** is a medium-sized, slender antelope similar to the gazelle in build. The impala

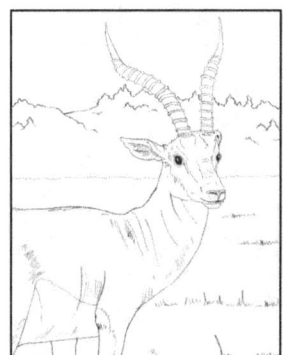

reaches 28 to 36 inches at the shoulder and weighs up to 170 pounds. Their glossy coat shows two-tone coloration – the reddish brown back and the tan flanks; these are in sharp contrast to the white underbelly. Facial features include white rings around the eyes and a light chin and snout. The long ears are tipped with black. Black streaks run from the buttocks to the upper hindlegs. The bushy white tail features a solid black stripe along the midline. The male has slender, lyre-shaped horns approximately 3-feet long. Active mainly during the day, the impala may be territorial depending upon the climate and geography. Three distinct social groups can be observed – the territorial males, bachelor herds, and female herds.

The **Key Deer** is unique to the Florida Keys. The smallest deer in North America, they are perfectly adapted to living in the wild; however, are not shy about approaching people looking

for handouts. The Key deer is endangered. Only the males grow antlers, which have a white velvet coating during growth. They generally resemble other white-tailed deer in appearance; reddish-brown or gray-brown in color. Sometimes called the "toy deer," the adult males, or bucks, weigh less than 70 pounds and stand only about 24 to 32 inches at the shoulder. Key deer easily swim between islands. The range of the Key deer originally encompassed all of the lower Florida Keys but is now limited to a stretch from Sugarloaf Key to Bahia Honda Key. They feed on over 150 types of plants but prefer mangroves and thatch palm berries.

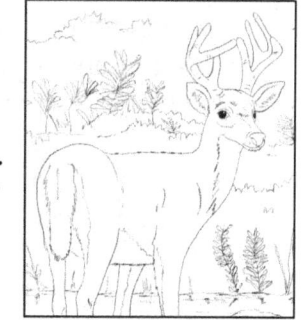

The **Koala** is a cuddly herbivorous marsupial native to Australia. Its closest living relatives are the wombats. The koala is found in coastal areas of the mainland's eastern and southern regions, inhabiting Queensland, New South Wales, Victoria, and South Australia. It is easily

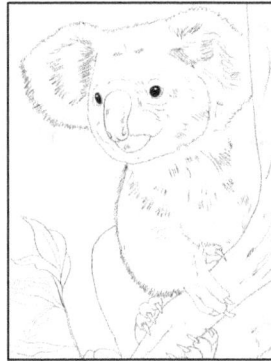

recognizable by its stout, tailless body and large head with round, fluffy ears, and large, spoon-shaped nose. The koala has a body length of 24 to 33 inches. The color of the hairy coat ranges from silver gray to chocolate brown. Koalas from the northern populations are typically smaller and lighter in color than their counterparts further south. Koalas typically inhabit open eucalypt woodlands, and the leaves of these trees make up most of their diet. Because their diet has limited nutritional and caloric content, koalas are largely sedentary and sleep up to 20 hours a day.

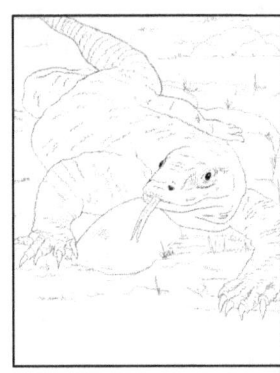

Komodo Dragon is the largest lizard on Earth. It is named after the island where it was discovered. Komodo is one of the 17,508 islands that compose the Republic of Indonesia. The largest verified wild specimen was 10.3 feet long and weighed 366 pounds. Their heads are square in shape. Young hatchling dragons eat insects and small lizards. Medium sized dragons eat rats and birds. Large adult dragons eat goats, pigs, deer, and smaller komodo dragons. They have been known to bring down horses and water buffalo. They have poor eyesight and hearing but have a keen sense of smell. The dragons can expand their jaws and swallow an entire fawn, a boar's head, or half a goat, in one gulp. After eating a large meal the dragons will settle down in the brush and may sleep for up to a week while digesting their food.

Leopard is one of the five "big cats" in the genus Panthera. It is a member of the family Felidae with a wide range in sub-Saharan Africa and parts of Asia. Fossil records found in Italy suggest that its pre-historic ancestors also occurred in Europe and Japan. The leopard has relatively short legs and a long body with a large skull. It is similar in appearance to the jaguar, but with a smaller, lighter physique. Its yellowish coat is marked with dark brown rosettes similar to those of the jaguar, but smaller and more densely packed, and do not usually have central spots. Both leopards and jaguars that have development of dark-colored pigment in the skin (the opposite of albinism) are known as black panthers. The leopard is distinguished by its well-camouflaged fur and unusual strength, as well as its ability to run at speeds of up to 36 mph. They are also known to be one of the best climbers in the cat family.

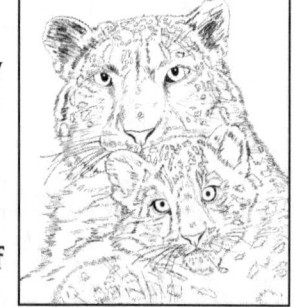

African Lions have excellent eyesight, good hearing and a keen sense of smell. They were once found throughout Africa, but they are now found mainly in sub-Sahara regions of southeastern Africa. In the wild, males need about 15 pounds of meat per day, while females need about 11 pounds. They hunt large to medium-sized animals, such as giraffe, water buffalo, zebra, wildebeest, wild hogs, and antelope. When a kill is made, the animals will gorge themselves because their meals are not certain or guaranteed. Lions live in a family or social group known as a pride headed by a dominant male. It is not unusual for lions to sleep up to 21 hours in a day, becoming active generally at night. Most hunting takes place during this active time. Lions, like most cats, are considered nocturnal.

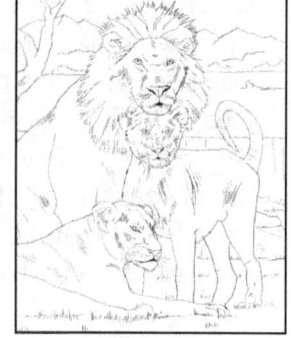

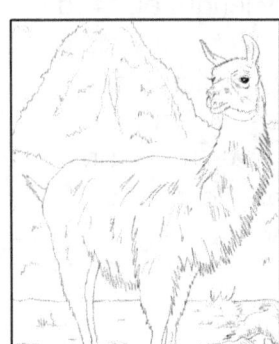

The **Llama** is a domesticated South American camelid, widely used as a meat and pack animal by Andean cultures since the Pre-Columbian era. The height of a full-grown, full-size llama is 5.6 to 5.9 feet tall at the top of the head and can weigh up to 450 pounds. They are very social animals and live with other llamas as a herd. The wool produced by a llama is very soft and lanolin-free. Llamas are intelligent and can learn simple tasks after a few repetitions. When using a pack, they can carry about 30 percent of their body weight for 8 miles. Llamas appear to have originated from the central plains of North America about 40 million years ago. They migrated to South America about three million years ago. By the end of the last ice age, camelids were extinct in North America. As domesticated animals, they were compared to and treated more like sheep, but their similarity to the camel is much more obvious.

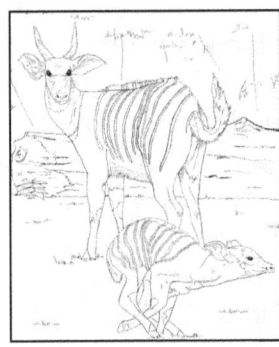

Lowland Nyala is a spiral-horned antelope native to East Africa, specifically in Ethiopia. The coat is rusty or rufous brown in females and juveniles but grows a dark brown or slate gray. Legs are tan. Nyala are noted for their striking white body striping and long, bushy tail with a white underside. Females and young males have ten or more white stripes on their sides. Only males have horns, 24 to 33 inches long and yellow-tipped. Stripes are reduced or absent in older males. Both males and females have a white chevron between their eyes, and a 16 to 22-inch long bushy tail white underside. The nyala feeds upon foliage, fruits, and grasses, with sufficient fresh water. A shy animal, it prefers water holes rather than open spaces.

The **Mandarin Duck** is found in East Asia. It is medium-sized and is closely related to the North American wood duck. The adult male is striking and unmistakable. It has a red bill, large white crescent above the eye and reddish face and whiskers. The breast is purple with two vertical white bars, and the flanks ruddy, with two orange "sails" at the back. The female is similar to female wood duck, with a white eye-ring and stripe running back from the eye, but is paler below, with a small white flank stripe. Both the males and females have crests, but the crest is more pronounced on the male. The male undergoes a molt after the mating season into eclipse plumage. When in eclipse plumage, the male looks similar to the female. Few other birds don such a dramatic and colorful costume as the male Mandarin Duck!

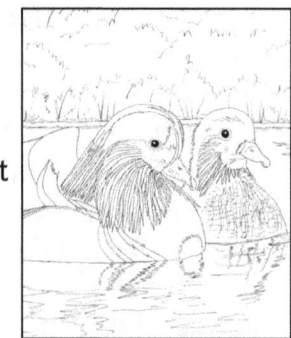

Mandrill is the world's largest monkey. Many people mistake the Mandrill for the Baboon but they are different. They do look similar to each other. The mandrill has an olive green or dark gray pelage with yellow and black bands and a white belly. Its hairless face has an elongated muzzle with distinctive characteristics, such as a red stripe down the middle and protruding blue ridges on the sides. It also has red nostrils and lips, a yellow beard and white tufts. The areas around the genitals and anus are multi-colored (red, pink, blue, scarlet, and purple). The males are darker than the females, and it is believed that females choose their mates based on the shade of coloring. Mandrills are found in southern Cameroon, Gabon, Equatorial Guinea, and Congo. They are found mostly in tropical rainforests. They live in very large groups. Mandrills have a diet consisting mostly of fruits and insects.

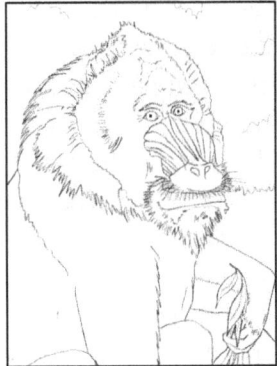

Meerkat is a small carnivoran in the mongoose family. Meerkats live in desert areas in groups of 30 to 50 members. A group of meerkats is called a "mob", "gang" or "clan". They have a long slender body and an added tail length of around nearly ten inches. The meerkat uses its tail to balance when standing upright, as well as for signaling. Its face tapers to a point at the nose, which is brown. The eyes always have black patches around them, and they have small black crescent-shaped ears. Like cats, meerkats have binocular vision, their eyes being on the front of their faces. At the end of each of a meerkat's "fingers" is a claw used for digging burrows and digging for prey. Claws are also used with muscular hindlegs to help climb trees. Meerkats have four toes on each foot and long slender limbs. The coat is usually peppered gray, tan, or brown with silver. They have short parallel stripes across their backs, extending from the base of the tail to the shoulders.

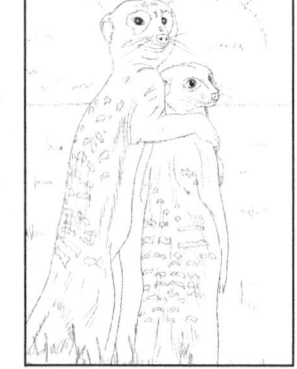

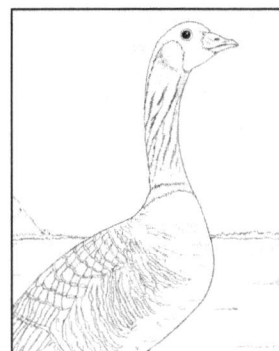

Nene is the world's rarest goose. It has endured a long struggle against extinction. During the 1940s, this beautiful species was almost wiped out. By 1957, when the Nene was named as Hawaii State Bird, rescue efforts were underway. They were bred in captivity to preserve the declining population and efforts made to re-establish their native habitat. It is thought that the nene evolved from the Canada goose, which most likely arrived on the Hawaiian islands about 500,000 years ago, shortly after the island of Hawai'i was formed. The nene is a medium-sized goose about 16 inches tall. Although they spend most of their time on the ground, they are capable of flight. Adult males have a black head and hindneck, buff cheeks and heavily furrowed neck. The neck has black and white diagonal stripes. The bill, legs, and feet are black. It has soft feathers under its chin.

Orangutan is found in the rainforests of Borneo and Sumatra. They are Asian species of extant great apes. Orangutans spend most of their time in trees. Their hair is typically reddish-brown, instead of the brown or black hair typical of chimpanzees and gorillas. Males and females differ in size and appearance. Dominant adult males have distinctive cheek pads. Younger males do not have these characteristics and resemble adult females. Orangutans are the most solitary of the great apes. Fruit is the most important component of an orangutan's diet; however, the apes will also eat vegetation, bark, honey, insects and even bird eggs. Orangutans are among the most intelligent primates; they use a variety of sophisticated tools and construct elaborate sleeping nests each night from branches and foliage.

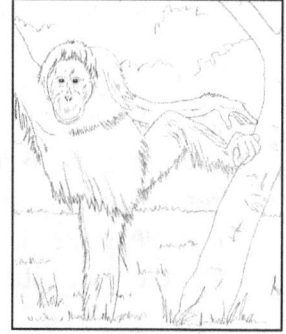

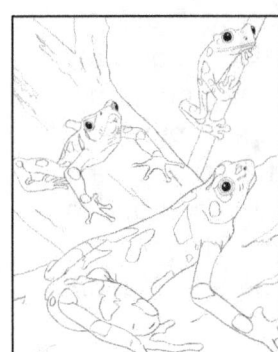

The **Panamanian Golden Frog** is a species of toad endemic to Panama. They inhabit the streams along the mountainous slopes of the Cordilleran cloud forests of west-central Panama. They are listed as critically endangered, but may, in fact, have been extinct in the wild since 2007. They are being bred in captivity to preserve the species. The Panamanian golden frog is a national symbol and is considered to be one of the most beautiful frogs in Panama. The skin color ranges from light yellow-green to bright gold; some have black spots on their backs and legs. Females are generally larger than males; reaching 2.5 inches in length with males less than 2 inches. The Panamanian golden frog has a variety of toxins. Their toxin is water-soluble and affects the nerve cells of anyone who comes in contact with it. The frogs use this toxin to protect themselves. Large doses can be fatal in 20 or 30 minutes.

The **Polar Bear** is a carnivorous bear whose native range lies largely within the Arctic Circle. It is a large bear, approximately the same size as the Kodiak bear. An adult male weighs around 1,500 pounds, while a female is about half that size. It has many body characteristics adapted for cold temperatures, for moving across snow, ice and open water, and for hunting seals, which make up most of its diet. Although most polar bears are born on land, they spend most of their time on the sea ice. Polar bears hunt their preferred food of seals from the edge of sea ice. Because of their dependence on the sea ice, polar bears are classified as marine mammals; they depend on the ocean as their main food source. The polar bear has a more elongated body build and a longer skull and nose. Their white fur coat can yellow with age.

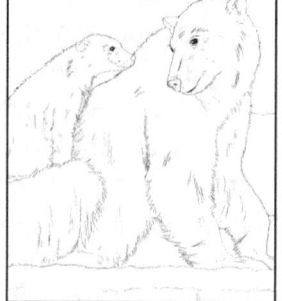

The **Pygmy Hippopotamus** is a smaller version of the closely related, and more well-known, Common Hippopotamus. The Pygmy Hippo is only half as tall and weighs less than one-fourth of its much larger cousin. While both are similar in some respects, such as a broad snout, a large mouth, a short, barrel-shaped body and short stocky legs, there are noticeable physical differences. The Pygmy Hippo's head is more rounded and the eyes are set on the side of the head rather than the front. Their smooth, almost hairless skin is greenish black above, fading to gray on the sides. It has well-separated toes with sharp nails, unlike the Hippopotamus which has webbed feet. The ears and large nostrils can be closed when the animal is under water.

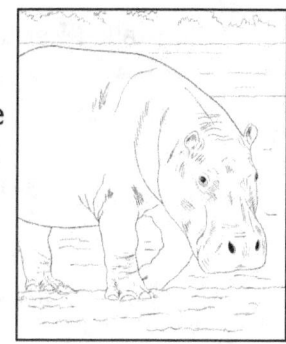

Diamondback Rattlesnake is considered the most dangerous venomous snake in North America. It is the heaviest though not the longest venomous snake in the Americas. The color pattern consists of a brownish, brownish-yellow, brownish-gray or olive earth tone, overlaid with a series of darker brown diamonds with slightly lighter centers. Each of these diamond-shaped blotches is outlined with a row of cream or yellowish scales. The belly is a yellowish or cream-colored, with diffused, dark mottling along the sides. The head has a dark stripe that extends from behind the eye backward and downwards to the lip; the back of the stripe touches the angle of the mouth. While not usually aggressive, they are large and powerful.

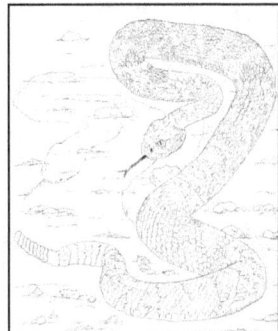

Red Wolf, also known as the Florida wolf or Mississippi Valley wolf, is native to the eastern United States. It is generally an intermediate between the coyote and gray wolf and is a reddish, tawny color. The red wolf is listed as a critically endangered species and is protected by law. Red wolves may have been the first New World wolf species encountered by European colonists. They were originally distributed from the Atlantic Ocean to central Texas. The red wolf was declared extinct in the wild by the mid-1900s and 14 of the survivors were selected to start a captive-bred population in 1974. Even though 63 captive animals were released in North Carolina in 1987, the number in the wild in 2015 was still fewer than 75 wolves. The red wolf is more sociable than the coyote but less so than the gray wolf. Besides the difference in color, the Red Wolf is more sparsely furred than the coyotes and gray wolf.

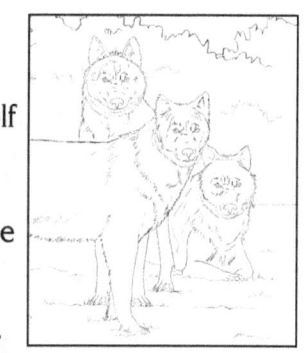

The name **Rhinoceros** is derived from two Ancient Greek words for "nose & horn." Often abbreviated rhino, the collective noun for a group of rhinoceroses is crash or herd. They are native to Africa and Southern Asia. Adult rhinoceros have no real predators in the wild, other than humans. Young rhinos can, however, fall prey to big cats, crocodiles, wild dogs, and hyenas. The rhino is characterized by large size and a thick protective skin, small brains for mammals this size, and a large horn. They generally eat leafy material, although their ability to ferment food in their hindgut allows them to subsist on more fibrous plant matter, if necessary. The African species of rhinoceros lack teeth at the front of their mouths, relying instead on their lips to pluck food. Rhinoceros are killed by humans for their horns, which are bought and sold on the black market, and which are used by some cultures for ornamental or traditional medicinal purposes. The color of this animal can range from yellowish brown to slate gray.

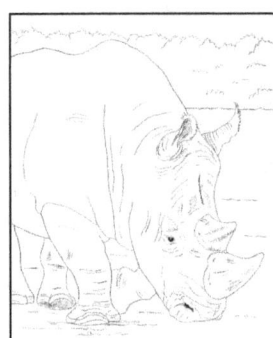

Ring-tailed Lemur is a large primate most recognized by its long, black and white ringed

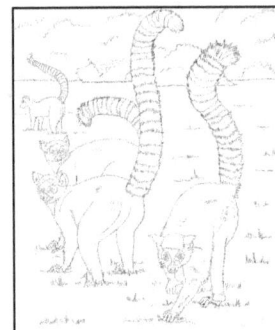

tail. It is endemic to the island of Madagascar. They inhabit gallery forests to spiny scrub in the southern regions of the island. It is omnivorous and most active in daylight hours. The ring-tailed lemur is highly social, living in groups of up to 30 individuals. It is also female dominant. To keep warm and reaffirm social bonds, groups will huddle together. The ring-tailed lemur will also sunbathe, sitting upright facing its underside, with its thinner white fur towards the sun. Like other lemurs, this species relies strongly on its sense of smell and marks its territory with scent glands. The males perform a unique scent marking behavior called spur marking. The ring-tailed lemur is listed as endangered.

Sandhill Crane is a large bird from the Platte River, on the edge of Nebraska's Sandhills on the American Plains. Adults are gray overall; during breeding, their plumage is usually much

worn and stained and looks ochre. Sandhill cranes have red foreheads, white cheeks, and long, dark, pointed bills. In flight, their long, dark legs trail behind, and their long necks keep straight. Immature birds have reddish-brown upperparts and gray underparts. These cranes frequently give a loud, trumpeting call, and they can be heard from a long distance. The cranes stand close together, calling in a synchronized and complex duet. Their large wingspans, over 7 feet, make them very skilled soaring birds, similar in style to hawks and eagles. They can stay aloft for many hours, requiring only occasional flapping of their wings and consequently expending little energy. Migratory flocks contain hundreds of birds. Sandhill

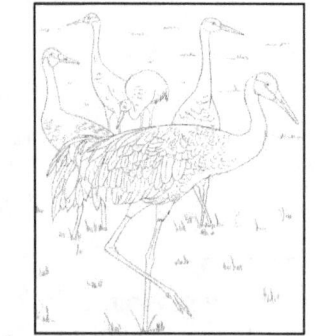

cranes fly south for the winter. In their wintering areas, they form flocks of over 10,000 birds.

The **Scarlet Macaw** is a large red, yellow, and blue South American parrot, a member of a

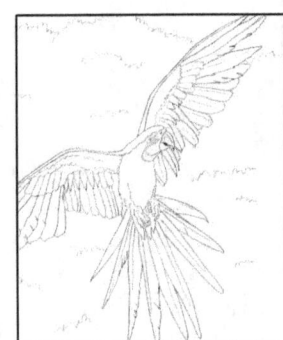

large group of tropical parrots called macaws. It is native to humid evergreen forests of South America, in a range that extends from Mexico to Peru. It has suffered from extinction through habitat destruction and capture for the parrot trade. It can still be found on the island of Coiba and is the national bird of Honduras. The Macaw is about 3-feet long, of which more than half is the long, pointed, tail. The scarlet macaw has a larger percentage of tail than the other macaws. The plumage is mostly scarlet, but the rump and tail feathers are light blue, the upper wings are yellow, the upper sides of the flight feathers of the wings are dark blue as are the ends of the tail feathers, and the undersides of the wing and tail flight feathers are dark red with metallic gold iridescence. Some have green in the wings.

Siamangs are small black apes. They are tailless with arms twice as long as a human's in proportion to body length. They hang by one long arm and use the other to gather fruit near the ends of branches. Siamangs are too quick for most predators although a few are taken by pythons. Siamangs climb by grasping with their hands and feet and leap as far as 45 feet from one tree branch to another. They mainly move by swinging arm over arm through the treetops, spanning twenty-foot gaps in the canopy with powerful arm pulls. The highly mobile thumb is set far back on the wrist and turned across the palm. Siamangs use their long fingers to hook rather than grasp the branches. When traveling on a large tree limb or on the ground, siamangs walk upright with the arms held overhead for balance.

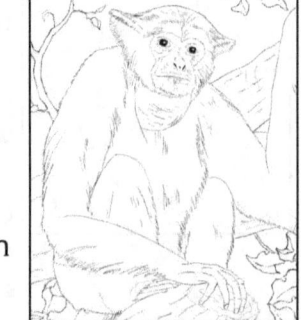

Sumatran Tiger is considered to be a critically endangered species. They are distinguished by heavy black stripes on their orange coats. Sumatran Tiger is darker than other subspecies and is the smallest. The fur on the sides of the face is a bit longer. Although the function of the fur is not exactly known, it may serve as a protection means when going through dense bushes. The Sumatran Tiger has white spots on the back of the ears that are believed to visually enlarge the size of the animal and serve as false eyes in the case that the predator is behind. Sumatran Tigers are one of the two cats that can be observed in water. Sometimes, they are seen near waterfalls and other water resources trying to cool themselves in hot weather. Moreover, they are good swimmers and are known to cross several rivers in search of prey. The species is equipped with webbed toes, which is another adaptation for life in the wild.

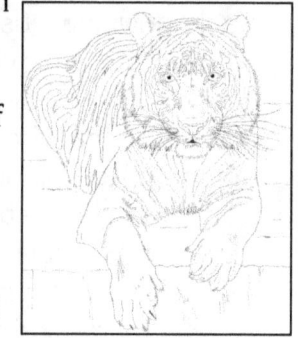

Sun Bear is found in tropical forest habitats of Southeast Asia. The Malayan sun bear is also known as the "honey bear" because of its voracious appetite for honeycombs and honey. The sun bear's fur is usually jet-black, short, and sleek with some under-wool; some sun bears are reddish or gray. A crescent-shaped pale patch is found on the breast that varies individually in color ranging from buff to dirty white. The skin is naked on the upper lip. The tongue is exceptionally long. The ears are small and round. The sun bear is the smallest of the bears. The muzzle is short and light colored, and in most cases, the white area extends above the eyes. The claws are large, curved, pointed, and sickle-shaped.

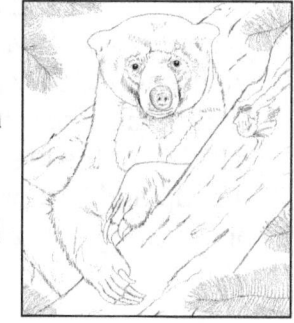

Visayan Warty Pig is a critically endangered species endemic to two of the Visayan Islands in the central Philippines. They only exist in the wild on the islands of Negros and Panay. The Visayan warty pig receives its name from the three pairs of small fleshy "warts" present on the visage of the boar. They live in groups of four to six. The diet of the pig mainly consists of roots, tubers, and fruits that can be found in the forest. Visayan warty pigs possess medium-sized, barrel-shaped bodies and short legs. They have short necks, longish heads, small eyes, prominent snouts ending in a disk-like nose, and tusks which are upturned lower canines. Sparse bristles cover their dark gray or black bodies (silvery or light-brown in adult males). They sport a tuft of dark hairs on the crowns of their heads and have a white stripe running across the bridge of the nose and along the jaw.

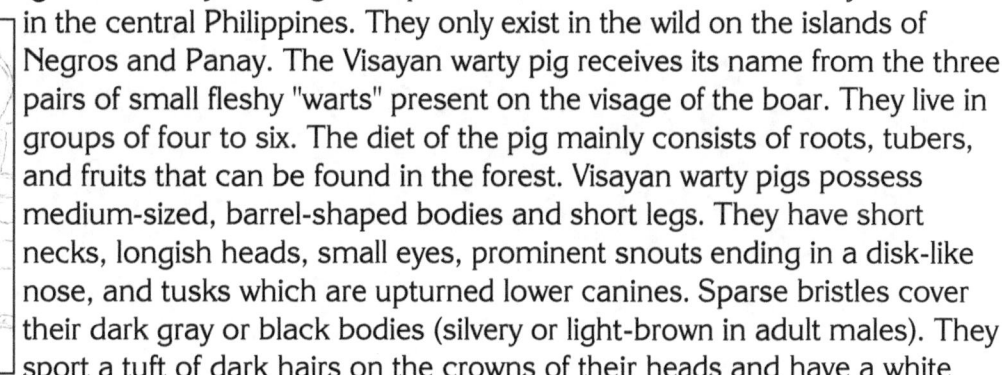

The **Wallaby** is a member of the kangaroo clan found primarily in Australia and on nearby islands. Wallabies are marsupials or pouched mammals. Their young are born tiny, helpless, and undeveloped. They immediately crawl into their mothers' pouches where they continue to develop for a couple of months after birth. Wallabies are typically small to medium-sized mammals, but the largest can reach 6 feet from head to tail. They have powerful hind legs they use to bound along at high speeds and jump great distances. The Wallaby fur ranges from reddish-brown to gray, with a lighter underside and accent colors around the face. These marsupials also have large and powerful tails used for balance. Wallabies are herbivores, and the bulk of their diet is grasses and plants. Their elongated faces leave plenty of jaw room for the large, flat teeth necessary to chew their vegetarian meals.

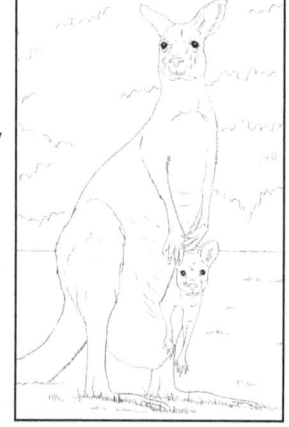

The **Zebra** is closely related to horses and donkeys, but the zebra is best known for its black and white striped body. In fact, zebra stripe patterns are unique to each individual, just as fingerprints are for humans. They are herbivorous and primarily eat a variety of grasses. Plains zebra is found on the savannas from Sudan to northern Zimbabwe in eastern Africa. Grevy's zebras are primarily restricted to parts of northern Kenya. Mountain zebras occur in southwestern Africa with cape mountain zebras in South Africa and Hartmann's mountain zebras in Namibia and Angola. Zebras as very social animals and live in large groups called harems consisting of one stallion and several mares. Zebras sleep standing up, and only when they are in groups that can warn them of danger. As a zebra grazes, it uses its sharper front teeth to bite the grass, and then uses its duller back teeth to crush and grind. Zebras are constantly on the move to find fresh grass and water. Sometimes they gather in huge herds of thousands as they migrate to better feeding grounds. When chased, a zebra will zig-zag from side to side, making it more difficult for the predator to attack. When cornered, the zebra will rear up and kick or bite its attacker. Zebras have excellent eyesight. In addition to superb eyesight and hearing, zebras also have acute senses of smell and taste.

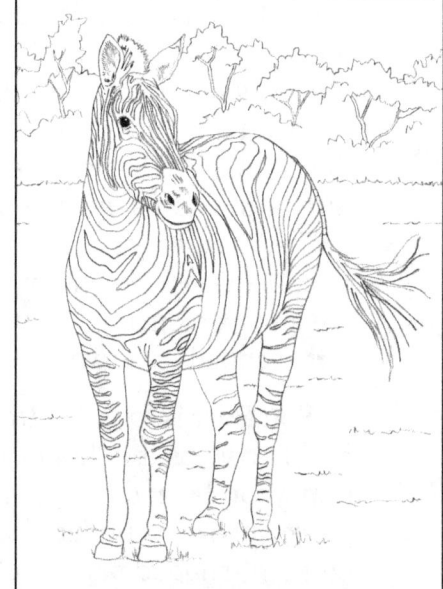